First World War
and Army of Occupation
War Diary
France, Belgium and Germany

56 DIVISION
Divisional Troops
Divisional Signal Company
1 October 1914 - 31 May 1919

WO95/2942/4

The Naval & Military Press Ltd
www.nmarchive.com
Published in association with The National Archives

Published by

The Naval & Military Press Ltd

Unit 10 Ridgewood Industrial Park,

Uckfield, East Sussex,

TN22 5QE England

Tel: +44 (0) 1825 749494

www.naval-military-press.com

www.nmarchive.com

This diary has been reprinted in facsimile from the original. Any imperfections are inevitably reproduced and the quality may fall short of modern type and cartographic standards.

© Crown Copyright
Images reproduced by permission of The National Archives, London, England, 2015.

Contents

Document type	Place/Title	Date From	Date To
Heading	WO95/2942/4		
Heading	56th Division 56th Divl Signal Corps Feb 1916-May 1919		
War Diary	Ipswich	11/02/1916	12/02/1916
War Diary	Southampton	12/02/1916	12/02/1916
War Diary	Havre	13/02/1916	15/02/1916
War Diary	Havre Rest Camp No 5	13/02/1916	13/02/1916
War Diary	Longpre	16/02/1916	16/02/1916
War Diary	Hallincourt	17/02/1916	27/02/1916
War Diary	Domart	28/02/1916	16/03/1916
War Diary	Le Cauroy	17/03/1916	31/03/1916
Heading	Signal Coy Vol III		
War Diary	Le Caruoy	01/04/1916	30/04/1916
Miscellaneous	To The Officer i/c Adjutant Generals Officer	31/05/1916	31/05/1916
War Diary	Le Cauroy	01/05/1916	05/05/1916
War Diary	Henu	06/05/1916	30/06/1916
War Diary	Souastre	30/06/1916	03/07/1916
War Diary	Henu	04/07/1916	31/07/1916
Heading	56th Divisional Engineers 56th Divisional Signal Company R.E. August 1916		
War Diary	Henu	01/08/1916	21/08/1916
War Diary	Doullens	22/08/1916	22/08/1916
War Diary	Fhroun-Le-Grand	23/08/1916	23/08/1916
War Diary	St Riquier	24/08/1916	31/08/1916
Heading	56th Divisional Engineers 56th Divisional Signal Company R.E. September 1916		
War Diary	St Riquier	01/09/1916	03/09/1916
War Diary	Corbie	04/09/1916	04/09/1916
War Diary	Longpre	04/09/1916	04/09/1916
War Diary	Corbie	04/09/1916	05/09/1916
War Diary	Fork Tree	06/09/1916	06/09/1916
War Diary	Billons Farm	07/09/1916	15/09/1916
War Diary	German Trench	16/09/1916	21/09/1916
War Diary	Billon Farm	22/09/1916	29/09/1916
War Diary	German Trench	30/09/1916	30/09/1916
Diagram etc	Communications Of Y.E.F		
Diagram etc	Circuit Diagram Of Y.E.F		
Diagram etc	Circuit Diagram		
Diagram etc	Diagram		
Operation(al) Order(s)	56th Divisional Order No. 33	07/09/1918	07/09/1918
Miscellaneous	Visual Instructions		
Operation(al) Order(s)	56th Divisional Order No. 36	12/09/1918	12/09/1918
Miscellaneous	Signalling Instructions	14/09/1918	14/09/1918
Heading	Headquarters 56th Division Herewith War Diary For The Month Of October Vol 9		
War Diary	German Wd	01/10/1914	10/10/1914
War Diary	Citadel	11/10/1914	11/10/1914
War Diary	Corbie	12/10/1914	12/10/1914
War Diary	Belloy Sur Somme	13/10/1914	20/10/1914
War Diary	Hallencourt	21/10/1914	23/10/1914

War Diary	Longpre	24/10/1916	24/10/1916
War Diary	Lestrem	25/10/1916	28/10/1916
War Diary	Le Gourgue	29/10/1916	31/12/1916
Heading	Headquarters 56th Div Herewith War Diary For January 1917		
War Diary	La Gourgue	01/01/1917	31/01/1917
Diagram etc	Diagram		
Heading	Headquarters 56th Div Herewith War Diary For Month Of February 1917		
War Diary	La Gorgue	01/02/1917	28/02/1917
Heading	Headquarters 56 Div Herewith War Diary For Month Of March 1917		
War Diary	La Gorgue	01/03/1917	05/03/1917
War Diary	St Venant	06/03/1917	06/03/1917
War Diary	Pernes	07/03/1917	07/03/1917
War Diary	Le Gauroy	08/03/1917	17/03/1917
War Diary	Simencourt	18/03/1917	18/03/1917
War Diary	Beaumetz	19/03/1917	09/04/1917
War Diary	Achicourt	09/04/1917	19/04/1917
War Diary	Couin	20/04/1917	25/04/1917
War Diary	Hauteville	26/04/1917	26/04/1917
War Diary	Walrus	27/04/1917	29/04/1917
War Diary	Arras	30/04/1917	21/05/1917
War Diary	Warlus	22/05/1917	24/05/1917
War Diary	Habarcq	25/05/1917	31/05/1917
Diagram etc	Diagram		
Heading	Headquarters 56 Div Herewith War Diary For June		
War Diary	Habarcq	01/06/1917	11/06/1917
War Diary	Arras	12/06/1917	22/06/1917
Diagram etc	56th Divisional Signal		
War Diary	Arras	23/06/1917	04/07/1917
War Diary	Le Cauroy	05/07/1917	23/07/1917
War Diary	Arques	24/07/1917	24/07/1917
War Diary	Eperlecques	25/07/1917	31/07/1917
Heading	Headquarters 56 Div Here With War Diary For August 1917		
War Diary	Eperlecques	01/08/1917	05/08/1917
War Diary	Noordpeen	06/08/1917	06/08/1917
War Diary	Reninghelst	07/08/1917	11/08/1917
War Diary	H 27 b 6.8	12/08/1917	18/08/1917
War Diary	Reninghelst	19/08/1917	24/08/1917
War Diary	Eperlecques	25/08/1917	30/08/1917
War Diary	Fremicourt	31/08/1917	31/08/1917
Diagram etc	56 Divisional Signal Compy Ret		
War Diary	Fremicourt	01/09/1917	30/09/1917
Diagram etc	Diagram		
War Diary	Fremicourt	01/10/1917	31/10/1917
Heading	HQrs. 56 Div Herewith War Diary for November		
War Diary	Fremicourt	18/11/1917	30/11/1917
Heading	Headquarters 56 Div Herewith War Diary For December		
War Diary	Fremicourt	01/12/1917	02/12/1917
War Diary	Fosseux	03/12/1917	04/12/1917
War Diary	Roclincourt	05/12/1917	31/12/1917
Diagram etc	56 Div Sigs Circuit Diagram		
War Diary	Victory Camp	01/01/1918	01/01/1918

War Diary	Roclincourt	01/01/1918	09/01/1918
War Diary	Villers Chatel	10/01/1918	31/01/1918
Heading	Headquarters 56th Divn Herewith War Diary For The Month Of February 1918		
War Diary	Villers Chatel	01/02/1918	20/02/1918
War Diary	Victory Camp Roclincourt G3B73	12/02/1918	28/02/1918
Diagram etc	Amplifier, Power Buzzer & Wireless Communications Oppy And Gavrelle Sectors 56th Div		
Diagram etc	Visual, D.R.L.S. Pigeons, Runner Posts		
Diagram etc	Circuit Pilot Diagram 56 Divisional Signal Coy		
Heading	War Diary 56th Divisional Signal Company R.E. March 1918		
War Diary	Victory Camp	01/03/1918	01/03/1918
War Diary	Rocklincourt	01/03/1918	01/03/1918
War Diary	Victory Camp	02/03/1918	17/03/1918
War Diary	Rocklincourt	17/03/1918	25/03/1918
War Diary	Victory Camp	26/03/1918	26/03/1918
War Diary	Rocklincourt	27/03/1918	30/03/1918
War Diary	Ack	31/03/1918	31/03/1918
Heading	56th Divisional Engineers 56th Divisional Signal Company R.E. April 1918		
War Diary	Acq	01/04/1918	06/04/1918
War Diary	Warlus	07/04/1918	30/04/1918
Diagram etc	56 Divn Diagram of Buried Routes		
Diagram etc	56 Divn Diagram of Buried Route		
War Diary	Warlus	01/05/1918	31/05/1918
Diagram etc	Local System		
War Diary	Warlus	01/06/1918	30/06/1918
Miscellaneous	56th Division	08/08/1918	08/08/1918
Miscellaneous	A Form Messages And Signals.		
War Diary	Warlus	01/07/1918	14/07/1918
War Diary	Roellecourt	15/07/1918	17/07/1918
War Diary	Villers Chatel	18/07/1918	01/08/1918
War Diary	Warlus	02/08/1918	17/08/1918
War Diary	Le Cauroy	18/08/1918	21/08/1918
War Diary	Bavincourt	22/08/1918	22/08/1918
War Diary	Blaireville	23/08/1918	26/08/1918
War Diary	Boisleux-St-Marc	27/08/1918	31/08/1918
War Diary	Boisleux-St. Marc S11a5.5 Sheet 51B	01/09/1918	08/09/1918
War Diary	Fosses Farm N12a 0.4	09/09/1918	26/09/1918
War Diary	V3b1.8	26/09/1918	04/10/1918
War Diary	Villers-Lez-Cagnicourt	04/10/1918	15/10/1918
War Diary	Etrun	16/10/1918	30/10/1918
War Diary	Basseville	31/10/1918	01/11/1918
War Diary	Monchaux	02/11/1918	03/11/1918
War Diary	Famars	04/11/1918	04/11/1918
War Diary	Saultain	04/11/1918	06/11/1918
War Diary	Sebourg	07/11/1918	08/11/1918
War Diary	Fayt Le Franc	09/11/1918	28/11/1918
War Diary	Harveng	29/11/1918	31/12/1918
Miscellaneous	Signal Coy Vol II		
War Diary	Harveng	01/01/1919	31/01/1919
War Diary	Harveng (Belgium)	01/02/1919	28/02/1919
War Diary	Harveng	01/03/1919	16/03/1919
War Diary	Harveng Belgium	17/03/1919	28/03/1919
War Diary	Jemappes Belgium	29/03/1919	31/03/1919

War Diary	Jemappes	01/04/1919	30/04/1919
War Diary	Jemappes	01/05/1919	18/05/1919
War Diary	Antwerp	19/05/1919	26/05/1919
War Diary	Tilbury	28/05/1919	28/05/1919
War Diary	Bulford	29/05/1919	31/05/1919

WO 95/2942/4

56TH DIVISION

56TH DIVL SIGNAL CORPS
FEB 1916-MAY 1919

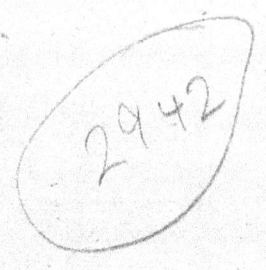
2942

Army Form C. 2118.

WAR DIARY
or
INTELLIGENCE SUMMARY
(Erase heading not required.)

56th Div. Signal Coy RE(TF)(1)

Hour, Date, Place	Summary of Events and Information	Remarks and references to Appendices
5PM/11/2 IPSWICH	Lieut VAC Cleary reported for duty. Authority War Office Telegram 3107 AAZ eighth. Signed PRACTICIAN LONDON	QK QK
3.30AM/12/2 IPSWICH	56th Div Sig Co RE TF entrained for SOUTHAMPTON authority Qz 419 Feb 9th	QK
6.30PM/12/2 SOUTHAMPTON	Sig Coy left Southampton	QK
4.0AM/13/2 HAVRE	Disembarked	QK
11AM/13/2 HAVRE REST CAMP No 5	Arrived at Rest Camp	QK
11AM/13/14/2 HAVRE RE No 5	Motor Lorry & 4 men departed by road HALLENCOURT	QK
2AM/15/2 HAVRE	Company entrained. 6.45.Am (departed)	QK
6AM/16/2 LONGPRÉ	Company detrained	QK
10.30PM/16/2	Arrived at HALLINCOURT Reported to 56th Division H.Q.	QK
17/2 HALLINCOURT	NIL	QK
18/2 Hallencourt	NIL	QK
19/2 Hallencourt	NIL	QK

Command Major RE to Division
OC Signals 56th Division

Army Form C. 2118.

WAR DIARY
or
INTELLIGENCE SUMMARY

(Erase heading not required.)

56 DIV SIGNAL COY RE (TF) (2)

Hour, Date, Place	Summary of Events and Information	Remarks and references to Appendices
20/2 HALLINCOURT	NIL	QK
21/2 HALLINCOURT	NIL	QK
22/2 HALLINCOURT	60 NCO's + men from Brigades reported for Divisional Signal School.	QK
4 PM		
9 PM HALLINCOURT	Telegram received from 6th Corps Signals directing Lt CLERY to report to 36th Div.	QK
23/2 HALLINCOURT	Att 3 SAPPERS from 167th RQE reported for instruction at SIGNAL SCHOOL	QK
	Lt CLERY departed as per orders	QK
24/2 HALLINCOURT 9.30 AM	All NCO. & MEN attached to Signal School returned to their units as per confidential instructions from Q.S.	QK
2.30 PM	nil	QK
25/2 HALLINCOURT	NIL	QK
26/2 HALLINCOURT		QK
27/2 HALLINCOURT 9.25 AM	Signal Coy departed by Route march to DOMART arriving at 4 PM 27/2/16	QK
28/2 DOMART	NIL	QK

Q Kennard Major RE
OC 56th DIV. SIGNAL COY RE(TF).

Army Form C. 2118.

56th Divisional Signal Coy
RE (TF)
3

WAR DIARY
or
INTELLIGENCE SUMMARY

(Erase heading not required.)

Instructions regarding War Diaries and Intelligence Summaries are contained in F.S. Regs., Part II. and the Staff Manual respectively. Title pages will be prepared in manuscript.

Hour, Date, Place	Summary of Events and Information	Remarks and references to Appendices
1/3/16 Domart	Nil	GK
2/3/16 Domart	Nil	GK
3/3/16 Domart 2 PM	60 NCO's & Men Reported for Divisional Signal School.	GK
4/3/16 Domart	2 Other ranks reported as re-inforcements. Sapper Target C.F. Sapper Gorod J.	GK
5/3/16 Domart	Nil	GK
6/3/16 Domart	Nil	GK
7/3/16 Domart	Nil	GK
8/3/16 Domart 10 PM	2nd Lt. G. H. Eyton reported for duty from 3RD LINE.	GK
9/3/16 Domart	Nil	GK
10/3/16 Domart	Nil	GK
11/3/16 Domart	2 Motor Cyclists (Cpls FISHER J (77863) LEVER S.C. 77350 Reported for duty from Signal Depot.	GK

Gordon Kennard
Major RET
OC Signals 56th Div

Army Form C. 2118.

WAR DIARY
or
INTELLIGENCE SUMMARY

(Erase heading not required.)

56th Divisional Signal Coy RE (TF)

Hour, Date, Place	Summary of Events and Information	Remarks and references to Appendices
12.3.16 HOMART 9.15 AM	Signal Coy moved by route march to DOULLENS. arriving at 4 P.M.	G.K.
13.3.16 DOULLENS	NIL	G.K.
14.3.16 "	NIL	G.K.
15.3.16 "	Sapper Travis Rgt No 14830 + Driver Robinson Rgt No 25790 reported from Signal Depot	G.K. G.K.
16.3.16 "	Signal Coy moved by route march to Le CAROY	G.K.
	Corp Fisher & Rgt No 77863 + Corp Lever Rgt No 77350 returned to Signal Depot	G.K.
17.3.16 Le Caroy	nil	G.K.
18.3.16 "	nil	G.K.
19.3.16 "	nil attended Conference called by ADAS 6th Corps of Div Sig Officers at 15 1h 9m	G.K.

Army Form C. 2118.

WAR DIARY
or
INTELLIGENCE SUMMARY

(Erase heading not required.)

5-6th Divisional Signal Coy
RE 3 F

Instructions regarding War Diaries and Intelligence Summaries are contained in F. S. Regs., Part II. and the Staff Manual respectively. Title pages will be prepared in manuscript.

Hour, Date, Place	Summary of Events and Information	Remarks and references to Appendices
20. 3. 16 LE CAROY	visited 5th Divisional Front	9K.
21 " " 16 "	nil	9K
22 " 3 " 16 "	nil	9K
23 " 3 " 16 "	DDAS. visited 56th Signals	9K
24 " 3 " 16 "	nil	
25 " 3 " 16 "	nil	9K
26 " 3 " 16 "	nil	9K
27 " 3 " 16 "	One cable detachment & half a Bde Section. Composed as under attached to 14th & 5th DIVISION. VIDE IIIV Order G 39/4	
	14 DIV 4 NCO 10 OR 5 DIV 8 NCO's 15 OR.	9K
	6 OR. + 2 Wireless sets reported for duty vide DDAS order 3rd Army NG/272 26/3/16	
	No STK/15 Privates ASBRIDGE N Private BARTLE G E 2939 Y M 9K
	25/4 " AYRES PG-L " SPOONER W 8859 "
	@ 6553 " McKENZIE I J STATION OXBY F 16847 STATION 9K
	Egerton Kennard
	O C Cos 56 a Major RE

1247 W 3299 200,000 (E) 8/14 J.B.C. & A. Forms/C. 2118/11.

Army Form C. 2118.

WAR DIARY
or
INTELLIGENCE SUMMARY

(Erase heading not required.)

56th Divisional Signal Coy
R E T F

Hour, Date, Place	Summary of Events and Information	Remarks and references to Appendices
27.3.1916 LE CAUROY	Sap. MONK Rgt. No 58511 reported for duty from Signal Depôt	G.K.
28.3.1916 "	Personnel & 2 Wireless Sets attached to 6th Corps for Duty vide Order HQ 6th Corps Q x 10/4. Six NCO & men departed for GIVENCHY for a Gas Course (5 days)	G.K. G.K.
29.3.16 "	Personnel & 2 Wireless Sets sent to VI Corps.	G.K.
30.3.16 "	Nil	G.K.
31.3.16 "	Rgt No 77794 Driver Dash H. Rgt No 77879 Sapper Barham A. Rgt No 81899 Pnr Barton J A reported for duty from Signal Depot.	G.K.

Gordon Kennard
major RE
O.C. 56 Divisional Signal
Coy. R E (T F)

56

Signal Coy

Vol III

Army Form C. 2118.

WAR DIARY
or
INTELLIGENCE SUMMARY

(Erase heading not required.)

56th Divisional Signal Coy

Hour, Date, Place	Summary of Events and Information	Remarks and references to Appendices
1.4.16 Le CARDY.	Nil.	
2.4.16 " "	One cable detachment & half a Bde section Returned from 14th & 5th Division One cable detachment & 7 Bde Section NCO & men departed for 5th Division	GK GK GK
3.4.16 " "	7 NCO's & men from Bde Section & 4 Lance Corporals from HQ & No 1 departed for 14 Division 25 O.R. returned to their units from Divisional Signalling School Attended Conference at 14th Div called by B.G. G.S. VI CORPS 2nd Lt Barker attached to 14th Division	GK GK GK GK GK
4.4.16	Nil	GK

Gordon Kennard Major RE
OC 56th Divisional Signal Coy

Army Form C. 2118.

WAR DIARY
or
INTELLIGENCE SUMMARY

56th Divisional Signal Coy

(Erase heading not required.)

Instructions regarding War Diaries and Intelligence Summaries are contained in F. S. Regs., Part II. and the Staff Manual respectively. Title pages will be prepared in manuscript.

Hour, Date, Place	Summary of Events and Information	Remarks and references to Appendices
5.4.16 Le Cauroy	Attended Conference called by DDAS VI Corps.	O.K.
6.4.16 Le Cauroy	NIL.	O.K.
7.4.16 Le Cauroy	Sgt Morris & 3 OR attached to 168 Bde Sig Section for duty	O.K.
8.4.16 Le Cauroy	7 NCO & men from B02 Section & 4 LC from HQ Section returned from 14th Div.	O.K.
	Lt Barber returned from 14th Div	O.K.
	Lt Carpenter & 6 OR from No 3 Section departed for 14th Div.	O.K.
	6 OR departed for 14 Div from HQ Section	O.K.
9.4.16 Le Cauroy	NIL	O.K.

Gorton Kennard
Major RE
OC Signals 56th Division

Army Form C. 2118.

56 Divisional Signal Coy

WAR DIARY
or
INTELLIGENCE SUMMARY

(Erase heading not required.)

Hour, Date, Place	Summary of Events and Information	Remarks and references to Appendices
10: 4: 16 LE CAUROY	6 Bat signallers attending School departed for Third Army WIRELESS Course	
11: 4: 16	NIL	
12: 4: 16 LE CAUROY	2 Instrument repairers Sap. KING E. & Sap E S Thorington departed for temp attachment to 6th CORPS SIGNALS	O.K. O.K.
13: 4: 16	NIL	O.K. O.K.
14: 4: 16 LE CAUROY	M/2 100439 Pte ALLNUTT reported for duty from 1st Base M T DEPOT M/2 148137 Pt Smith G reported for duty from Amm Sub Park	O.K. O.K.

Gordon Kennard
Major RE
O C Signals / 56th Division

Army Form C. 2118.

10

WAR DIARY
or
INTELLIGENCE SUMMARY.
(Erase heading not required.)

56th Div Signal Coy R.E. (PETE)

Instructions regarding War Diaries and Intelligence Summaries are contained in F. S. Regs., Part II. and the Staff Manual respectively. Title pages will be prepared in manuscript.

Place	Date	Hour	Summary of Events and Information	Remarks and references to Appendices
LE CAUROY	15/4/16		Sapper Harding CH 1607 reported for duty (returned from Signal Depot)	G.K.
			Lt Carpenter & 12 OR returned from 14th Div. Remainder of Sig Setups returned to 14th Div. Driver Greenwood H.T.921 reported for duty from 1st Base HT Depot.	G.K. G.K.
LE CAUROY	16/4/16		Nil.	G.K.
LE CAUROY	17/4/16		Lt Maslin Lt Fox 12 Artillery 1 nco man 6 OR from No 4 Section departed for 14th Div	G.K.
			60 Signallers from Infantry Battalions 3 Instructors from Bde sections L8 Artillery Signallers reported for Course of Instruction att 2nd Divisional Signalling Course	G.K.
LE CAUROY	18/4/16		2nd Lieut C W Arthur reported for duty from 37th DIVISION	G.K.

Gordon Kennard
Major R.E.
O C Signals 56 Division

T.131. Wt. W708-776. 500000. 4/15. Sir J. C. & S.

Army Form C. 2118.

WAR DIARY
or
INTELLIGENCE SUMMARY.
(Erase heading not required.)

5-6 Divisional Signal Coy

Place	Date	Hour	Summary of Events and Information	Remarks and references to Appendices
Le Cauroy	19th	–	Nil	–
"	20th	"	Nil	–
"	21st	–	Private Oates L/Cpl. Wilson No. IMY2/075593 ASC mt reported for duty	–
"	"	–	Lt Maslin & Sgt Gornell returned from attachment to 14th Div	–
"	22nd	–	nil	–
"	23rd	–	nil	–
Le Cauroy	24th	–	DAS visited Company	–
"	25th	–	All ranks attached to 14th Div returned for duty	–
"	26th	–	nil	–
"	27th	–	1 Officer & 12 OR TMB returned to their units	–
"	28th	–	nil	–
"	29th	–	nil	–
"	30th	–	nil	–

1 Officer & 12 OR (TMB) reported for 1 weeks conference — gr

gr gr gr gr gr gr gr gr gr gr gr gr

Gordon Kennard
OC Signals
56th Division

To The Officer
i/c Adjutant-General's
Office

Herewith War Diary for
month ending 31/5/16.

Gordon Kennard
Major RE
Commdg 56th Divl Signals

56th DIVISIONAL
SIGNAL COMPANY,
R.E.
No. K227.
Date 31/5/16.

Army Form C. 2118.

WAR DIARY
or
INTELLIGENCE SUMMARY.
(Erase heading not required.)

56 Divisional Signal Coy RE

Place	Date	Hour	Summary of Events and Information	Remarks and references to Appendices
LE CAUROY	1/5/16		2nd Lieuts GYTON, ARTHUR, Carpenter, attended Divisional Gas Course at QLEVENCHY. O.C. Sigs called attended conference of 7th Corps L84 Division etc. 2 Wireless OR attached to VI Corps returned to duty 2 OR INSTRUMENT Repearers returned from VI Corps to duty	Q.K. Q.K. Q.K. Q.K.
LE CAUROY	2/5/16		O.C. Sigs Lt Smith, For Maslin attended gas course at QLEVENCHY. 3 Wireless OR attached VI Corps returned to duty	Q.K. Q.K.
LE CAUROY	3/5/16	5 PM	2 Cable detachments departed by route march to HENU with O.C. Sigs.	Q.K.
LE CAUROY	4/5/16		Lt S.E. Smith departed to HENU. O.C. Sigs returned to LE CAUROY	Q.K.
LE CAUROY	5/5/16		Remainder of Company moved by route march to HENU.	Q.K.

Army Form C. 2118.

WAR DIARY
or
INTELLIGENCE SUMMARY.   56 Divisional Signal Coy
(Erase heading not required.)

Instructions regarding War Diaries and Intelligence Summaries are contained in F. S. Regs., Part II. and the Staff Manual respectively. Title pages will be prepared in manuscript.

Place	Date	Hour	Summary of Events and Information	Remarks and references to Appendices
LECNURoy	5/5/16		All Artillery Signallers returned to their units. 2/Lt Egerton Can gave a L/c Hockley departed for Wireless Course with 3rd ARMY	9K 9K
HENU.	6/5/16	10 AM	Communications established as under. Divisional HQ opened at HENU	9K

[Diagram showing signal communications with locations: LA HAIE, SAILLY, SOUASTRE, BAYENCOURT, JUNCTION POLE HENU, YEF, YPH, YDF, GCO, with lines labelled G105, G105 A+B]

Army Form C. 2118.

WAR DIARY
or
INTELLIGENCE SUMMARY
(Erase heading not required.)

56 Div Signal Coy R.E.   14

Hour, Date, Place	Summary of Events and Information	Remarks and references to Appendices
7/5/16 Henu	Normal. Communications established to 169 Bde at HALLOY	O.K. O.K.
8/5/16 Henu	Situation Normal. Inspected Front	
9/5/16 "	Cuv communications Remainder of Coy reported from LE CAUROY	O.K.
10/5/16	Situation Normal	O.K.
11/5/16	Communication established 169 BDC Souvrir to BAYENCOURT 2nd Lieut ARTHUR & 10 O.R. from 168+ 169 Bde sections	
12/5/16	Working on Front Line communications Situation Normal	O.K. O.K.
13/5/16	Situation normal	O.K.

G Kennard
Major RE
O.C. Signals 56 Div

WAR DIARY
or
INTELLIGENCE SUMMARY

Army Form C. 2118.

56 DIV Signal Coy

Hour, Date, Place	Summary of Events and Information	Remarks and references to Appendices
14/5/16 Henu	Signal School terminated all men returned to their Battalions	O.K.
		O.K.
	Following men reported for Pigeon Service 1299 Private Hoyle A.J.	
	3362 Private Henson A.	O.K.
	4059 Rfn Barnard A.J.	O.K.
	4556 Pt Turnbull K.L.R.	O.K.
	3403 Pt Griffiths	O.K.
	3701 Rfn Brooks	O.K.
15/5/16 Henu	Attended Conference called by South Corps	O.K.

G Kennard
Major R.E.
O Signals 56 Div

Army Form C. 2118.

WAR DIARY
or
INTELLIGENCE SUMMARY.
(Erase heading not required.)

Instructions regarding War Diaries and Intelligence Summaries are contained in F.S. Regs., Part II. and the Staff Manual respectively. Title pages will be prepared in manuscript.

16

Hour, Date, Place	Summary of Events and Information	Remarks and references to Appendices
16/5/16 Henu	Electric Lighting Lorry received from GHQ	G.K.
17/5/16	Situation normal	G.K.
18/5/16	DAS visited Company	G.K.
19/5/16	Diagram of Communications to established during preceding week as overleaf	G.K.

Gordon Kennard
Major RE
O C Signals
56 Division

Army Form C. 2118.

WAR DIARY
or
INTELLIGENCE SUMMARY.
(Erase heading not required.)

Instructions regarding War Diaries and Intelligence Summaries are contained in F. S. Regs., Part II. and the Staff Manual respectively. Title pages will be prepared in manuscript.

Hour, Date, Place	Summary of Events and Information	Remarks and references to Appendices

[Diagram of signals communications network showing the following labelled nodes and connections:]

- MONDICOURT EXCH
- PAS
- GCO
- GUN PARK
- GRENAS
- TRW
- HENU — 56th YEF — 1st / 2nd [boxed unit symbol]
- FL.1
- DIV ARTY HQRS
- YDH COUIN
- YCG BAVINCOURT (37th DIV)
- LD/4th LONS
- FL.A
- 280th BDE ARTY
- BAYENCOURT R.E. DUMP
- FL.B
- 281st BDE ARTY
- LS (LONDON SCOTTISH)
- 5th CHESHIRES
- FT EDINBURGH FIELD Co
- SOUASTRE
- BDE HQRS. SAULTY-AU-BOIS

(73989) W4144—463. 400,000. 9/14. H.&J.Ltd. Forms/C. 2118/10.

Army Form C. 2118.

WAR DIARY
or
INTELLIGENCE SUMMARY. 56 Divisional Signal Coy
(Erase heading not required.)

Hour, Date, Place	Summary of Events and Information	Remarks and references to Appendices
20:5:16 HENU	New French digging scheme (Corn) for VII Corps commenced	OK
21:5:16	Lt Smith proceeded on seven days leave	OK
22:5:16	Private 95553 McKenzie W.J. from 13th R.F. reported for duty.	OK
23:5:16	Situation normal	OK
24:5:16	2nd Lieut C D'artois from 57 Div reported for a weeks attachment from England	OK
25:5:16	Working party of Signal Coys shelled at SAILLY-LE-BOIS no casualties	OK
	Operations new advanced trenches commenced. Communications established by 2nd Lieut H Barber 4&2 Section Signal Coy	OK

G Kennard Lt
Major OC 56 Divisional
Signal Coy

WAR DIARY
or
INTELLIGENCE SUMMARY

Army Form C. 2118

Place	Date	Hour	Summary of Events and Information	Remarks and references to Appendices
HENU	26/5/16		Operations again continued & completed (successfully) Total amount of cable buried in open trenches by Signal Coy for these operations equalled 30 miles.	G.K. G.K.
HENU	27/5/16		Situation normal. Cable winding apparatus which can twist 18-20 miles of cable per day inspected by Corps Commander, ADAS VII Corps etc.	G.K. G.K.
HENU	28/5/16		Situation normal. SOS call received at Signal Office (30*5*16) 12.30AM from 169 Bde retransmitted CRA & Corps Heavy Artillery etc.	G.K. G.K.
HENU	29/5/16			
HENU	30/5/16		Situation normal. Lt Smith SE reported (returned from leave)	G.K.

WAR DIARY
or
INTELLIGENCE SUMMARY

Army Form C. 2118.

Hour, Date, Place	Summary of Events and Information	Remarks and references to Appendices
31.5.16 Henu	A C D'ART & left to return to England	GK

Gordon Kennard
Major R.E.
O C Signals 6-6 Division

Army Form C. 2118.

WAR DIARY
or
INTELLIGENCE SUMMARY

(Erase heading not required.)

56 Divisional Signal Co RE

Vol 5

Hour, Date, Place	Summary of Events and Information	Remarks and references to Appendices
1.6.16 HENU	Situation Normal	GK
2.6.16 Henu	2nd Lieut H Barber departed for one weeks leave	GK
3.6.16 HENU	Situation normal	GK
4.6.16 HENU	Sapper WT Granger 1989 Sapper HM Vincent 1398 Sapper PF Cowan 1419 reported for duty as reinforcements	GK
5.6.16 Henu	Commenced communication trenches with 800 men working 3 hours per day	GK
6.6.16 Henu	Capt HH King POR reported for duty from 29th to 17th IV	GK
7.6.16 HENU	Situation Normal. 600 men digging at night under 2 Smith & 2 mo Lieut Arthurs	GK

G Kennard
Major RE O.C. Sigs

WAR DIARY
or
INTELLIGENCE SUMMARY

(Erase heading not required.)

Army Form C. 2118.

5-6 IV Signal Coy 2g

Hour, Date, Place	Summary of Events and Information	Remarks and references to Appendices
8.6.16 HENU	168 Bde relieved 169 Bde day & night trenches continued	OK
9.6.16 HENU	266 (Comp) S.M. arres reported for duty (Supernumerary) from 3RD LINE	OK OK
10.6.16 HENU	Situation Normal day & night trenches continued	OK
11.6.16 HENU	Situation normal Lance Corp Smith IIH 1064 Sapper Folks W 2039 reported for duty from Signal Depot 2nd Lt Barber returned from leave	OK OK
12.6.16 HENU	Situation normal	OK
13.6.16 HENU	Situation Normal	OK
14.6.16 "	Situation Normal	
15.6.16	Situation Normal Capt Lindsey Renton 14 London Rgt. attached for duty Sapper Groves WC no 3 Section wounded Gordon Kennard Major RE O C Sigs 56 Div	OK OK

Army Form C. 2118.

WAR DIARY
or
INTELLIGENCE SUMMARY

(Erase heading not required.)

5-6 Divisional Signal Coy

Instructions regarding War Diaries and Intelligence Summaries are contained in F.S. Regs., Part II. and the Staff Manual respectively. Title pages will be prepared in manuscript.

Hour, Date, Place	Summary of Events and Information	Remarks and references to Appendices
16.6.16 1/16 HENU	Situation normal	GK
17.6.16 1/16 HENU	"	GK
18.6.16 "	Situation normal	GK
19.6.16 "	Commenced burying lines in clay Trenches. Situation Normal	GK GK
20.6.16 "	as above. Situation normal Sapper Roe H 1687 reported for duty as reinforcements	GK GK
21.6.16 "		GK
22.6.16 "	Laying lines opening of new Report centre SOUASTRE. Establishing advanced BDE Report centres at HERPTERNE at KYC KYR taking lines forward for 168 BDE. SITUATION NORMAL	GK

Gordon Kennerell
Major RE OC Signals
56 Division

WAR DIARY
or
INTELLIGENCE SUMMARY

Army Form C. 2118.

24

Hour, Date, Place	Summary of Events and Information	Remarks and references to Appendices
23.6.16 HENU	Communication Trenches & Cable laying continued. Situation normal Filling in Trenches	GK
24.6.16 "	Operations commenced. SIGNAL Operations orders attached in sealed envelope. No K286.	GK
25.6.16 "	Bombardment continues. 600 men filled up Communication trench in Corps Area	GK
26.6.16 "	Bombardment continued. Cable trenchs being filled up & lines forwarded through	GK
27.6.16 "	Bombardment continued (as above)	GK
28.6.16 "	Signal HQ moved to SOUASTRE. Men returned as attack of enemy lines postponed	GK

Gretton Reinard Major
O.C Signals 56 Division

WAR DIARY
or
INTELLIGENCE SUMMARY

Army Form C. 2118.

(Erase heading not required.)

Hour, Date, Place	Summary of Events and Information	Remarks and references to Appendices
29th 6 · 16 HENU	Completion of Battle Headquarters SOUASTRE. Lines tested — found O.K.	Gordon Kennard
30th 6 · 16 HENU	Signal HQ moved to SOUASTRE Lineman posted as follows Left Bde. KYC. 2 LINEMAN. H. Corp Langley "Symons JT Right Bde ZPH. Bde Section Lineman Reserve Bde KYR. Baker Cpl Le Cpl Lockey Advanced Signal Exchange Lt Arthur Corp Walton Spr MacCurhes Cpl Penen Spres Taylor Treves Ross	

Army Form C. 2118.

WAR DIARY
or
INTELLIGENCE SUMMARY
(Erase heading not required.)

Instructions regarding War Diaries and Intelligence Summaries are contained in F.S. Regs., Part II. and the Staff Manual respectively. Title pages will be prepared in manuscript.

Hour, Date, Place	Summary of Events and Information	Remarks and references to Appendices
30.6.18. SODACTRE	During the evening of 30th 6/16 Lance Corp. Baker W.F. & Corp. Lockey P.G. continuously repaired Buried Cable under fire & maintained communication with the 168 Bde of Infantry	

Gordon Kennard
Major RE
OC Signals
56 Division

Army Form C. 2118.

WAR DIARY
or
INTELLIGENCE SUMMARY

(Erase heading not required.)

56 Divisional Signal Co^y R.E.

Instructions regarding War Diaries and Intelligence
Summaries are contained in F. S. Regs., Part II.
and the Staff Manual respectively. Title pages
will be prepared in manuscript.

Hour, Date, Place	Summary of Events and Information	Remarks and references to Appendices
7.30am 1.7.16 SOUASTRE	Attack commenced at 7.30 am. Enemies trenches up to their third line captured. Communication over No Mans Land difficult, to Signal Stations in extreme front good visual established once no mans land. Short DD messages received that evening the battalions withdrew to their own front line trenches	
2.7.16 SOUASTRE	168 Bde. established their Headquarters at SAILLY-AUX-BOIS. Communication established	G.K.
3.7.16 SOUASTRE	Situation normal. Artillery active. Signals clearing lines Communication trenches.	G.K.
4.7.16 HENU	Divisional HQ established at HENU 2pm. Signals engaged establishing Communication to FRON- QUEVILLERS for Bde move. Lines of 46 Division diverted + extended, otherwise situation normal	G.K.

Gordon Kennard
Major RE
OC Signals 56 Division

1247 W 3250 200,000 (E) 8/15 J.B.C. & A. Forms/C. 2118/11.

Army Form C. 2118.

56 Divisional Signal @ YRE

WAR DIARY
or
INTELLIGENCE SUMMARY
(Erase heading not required.)

Instructions regarding War Diaries and Intelligence Summaries are contained in F. S. Regs., Part II. and the Staff Manual respectively. Title pages will be prepared in manuscript.

Hour, Date, Place

Summary of Events and Information

Remarks and references to Appendices

[Hand-drawn signal communications diagram showing connections between stations including YEFR, KYC, KYR, QJ, HCOI, HCO6, RNR, ZPH L/T reporter, 8th Corps A. Dugout, 48th Div, with locations HEBUTERNE, SAILLY, SOURSTRE, HENU marked. Notes include "WIRE CUTTING GROUP R.F.A.", "ADVANCED HQRS SOUTHERN GROUP ARTY", "NORTHERN GROUP ART?", "SOUTHERN GROUP ART?", "MORSE LINE", "TO 46 DIV R.C.", "TO 48TH DIV", "TO 37TH DIV", and legend "56TH DIV MAIN ROUTES 1.2.3 ETC ANSWERED YEPRA YERRB LINES ETC FURTHER"]

E Kennard Major RE

Army Form C. 2118.

WAR DIARY
or
INTELLIGENCE SUMMARY

(Erase heading not required.)

56 Divisional Signal Coy RE

Instructions regarding War Diaries and Intelligence Summaries are contained in F. S. Regs., Part II. and the Staff Manual respectively. Title pages will be prepared in manuscript.

Hour, Date, Place	Summary of Events and Information	Remarks and references to Appendices
6.7.16 HENU	Took over Southern portion of 46th Div lines of Communication also. Between D 22 A/5 — E 28 A 39 Sheet 57 D adjusting extending & replacing these lines to meet requirements. Also Artillery Communications. Continuation of work as above	
7.7.16 HENU	Changes of Artillery groups, lines diverted.	✓K. ✓K. ✓K.
8.7.16 HENU	(1753 A/k/c Baily EA reinforcement from Signal Depot reported for duty originals in this coy. Establishing 8 lines of communication to LA HAYE FARM 36 B 83	✓K ✓K
9.7.16 HENU	All signal sections building 4 Pr air line route to SOUASTRE to take up extra front lines taken over 46 DIVISION Completed 2 PM Commenced work of clearing lines behind HIBUTERNE	

Edward Major RE O.C. 56 Division

Army Form C. 2118.

WAR DIARY
or
INTELLIGENCE SUMMARY
(Erase heading not required.)

56 Divisional Signal Co RE

Hour, Date, Place	Summary of Events and Information	Remarks and references to Appendices
10.7.16 HENU	168 Bde relieved 167 Bde. requested lines required to meet requirements. Bde HQ established at SOUASTRE opened 12 AM by 167 Bde. Opened office & requested lines.	GK
11.7.16 HENU	Situation normal. Replaced all ocd D5 Cable route from left Dug out FONQUEVILLERS & at BDE HQ at SHRINE by armoured & D5. Completed 5.30 PM	GK GK
12.7.16 HENU	(16160 A/Cpl Butcher C reported for duty from Signal Depot) Readjustment of Front line. 3 Bdes in. & their Groups of Artillery affiliated as follows. 168 SAILLY. 167 (CHA. DE. LA. HAYE 169 FONQUEVILLERS LINES of communications requested, extensions completed & Communication established	GK GK GK

G Kennard
Major RE
OC Signals 56 Division

Army Form C. 2118.

WAR DIARY
or
INTELLIGENCE SUMMARY

56 Divisional Signal Co. R.E.

(30)

(Erase heading not required.)

Hour, Date, Place	Summary of Events and Information	Remarks and references to Appendices
13.7.16 HENU	37 Division took over main LINE which necessitated our cutting out main Route No Guorion HENU to St AMAND. Changed there over, reestablished communications to meet new requirements	E.K.
14.7.16 HENU	Adjusting + making good. Situation normal	E.K.
15.7.16 HENU	HEADQTRS. 169 BDE. established at BIENVILLERS. Took over 37 Div communications. extended + readjusted lines to your direction to BIENVILLERS. Brought all new lines in to SOUASTRE REPORT CENTRE	E.K. E.K.

E Kinnard
Major R.E.
O C Signals 56 Division

Army Form C. 2118.

(31)

56 Div Signal Co. RE (TF)

WAR DIARY
or
INTELLIGENCE SUMMARY
(Erase heading not required.)

Hour, Date, Place	Summary of Events and Information	Remarks and references to Appendices
16.7.16 HENU	Lt S E Smith departed for duty with 29th Division vide Orders A Q E 48 56 Division	G.K
	Capt H H King departed for duty with 60th Division vide Orders X1319 56 DIV	G.K
17.7.16 HENU	Parties engaged on clearing new areas Com Trenches	G.K
	Establishing new lines to BIENVILLERS Clearing. Situation normal	G.K
18.7.16 HENU	(Reinforcements) 1642 Driver Skipper P.J. 37079 Sapper Egleson J. 151916 Sapper Richardson J.A 54013 Cpl McLetchie H.H) reported	G.K
19.7.16 HENU	3 Parties from 7th Corps & 20 men from 3RD ARMY reported for duty to help to clear dead wire from trenches	G.K

G Kennard
Major RE
OC Signals 56 Division

Army Form C. 2118. (32)

56 Divisional Signal Co. R.E.

WAR DIARY
or
INTELLIGENCE SUMMARY
(Erase heading not required.)

Instructions regarding War Diaries and Intelligence Summaries are contained in F. S. Regs, Part II. and the Staff Manual respectively. Title pages will be prepared in manuscript.

Hour, Date, Place	Summary of Events and Information	Remarks and references to Appendices
20.7.16 HENU	Situation Normal. Clearing area	GK
21.7.16 HENU	446 Sergt NIGHTINGALE ST 9 17515 Sap KNAPP AW wounded by shrapnell. 2nd Lieut ONASKIN H.I. reported for duty from Divisional rest station	GK GK
22.7.16 HENU	Line to WARLINGCOURT said clearing dead wires relaying armoured cable to KYE HIBBERT'S partly destroyed by shell fire	GK GK
23.7.16 HENU	Clearing area otherwise normal (1389 A/cr Batting reported for duty from Signal Depot)	GK
24.7.16 HENU 25.7.16 " 26.7.16 " 27.7.16 "	Relaying & making good armoured cable Bienvillers & HEBUTERNE. Clearing area & laying lines in trenches	GK

Gordon Kennard
Major RE OC Signals 56 Div

1247 W B260 200,000 (E) 8/15 J.B.C.&A. Form C. 2118 11.

Army Form C. 2118.

(33)

56 Divisional Signal Coy

WAR DIARY
or
INTELLIGENCE SUMMARY
(Erase heading not required.)

Instructions regarding War Diaries and Intelligence Summaries are contained in F. S. Regs., Part II. and the Staff Manual respectively. Title pages will be prepared in manuscript.

Hour, Date, Place	Summary of Events and Information	Remarks and references to Appendices
28.7.16 HENU	D.D.A.S. called to interview candidates for Commission Signal Service. Clearing area continued.	9/K
29.7.16 HENU	Clearing + renumbering main communication lines. Area clearing + making good all exchange dugouts	9/5
30.7.16 "		
31.7.16 "	168 Bde HQ changed Signal office to HQ SAILLY. Establishing lines + clearing	9/15

London Kenward
Major R.E.
OC Signal Coy
56 Division

56th Divisional Engineers.

56th DIVISIONAL SIGNAL COMPANY R. E.

AUGUST 1 9 1 6

Instructions regarding War Diaries and Intelligence
Summaries are contained in F. S. Regs., Part II.
and the Staff Manual respectively. Title pages
will be prepared in manuscript.

INTELLIGENCE SUMMARY

(Erase heading not required.)

5-6 Divisional Signal Coy R.E.T.F.

Hour, Date, Place	Summary of Events and Information	Remarks and references to Appendices
1.8.16 Henu	Situation normal	GK
2.8.16 "	" "	GK
3.8.16 "	" "	GK
4.8.16 "	" "	GK
5.8.16 "	" "	GK
6.8.16 "	" "	GK
7.8.16 Henu	2nd Lieut E Williams reported for duty from 3rd Line	GK
8.8.16 Henu	Situation normal	GK
9.8.16 Henu	Capt Lindsey Renton attached Temp from London Scottish departed for 11th Division	GK
10.8.16 Henu	Situation normal	GK
12.8.16 "	" "	GK
13.8.16 "	" "	GK
14.8.16 "	" "	GK
15.8.16 Henu	" "	GK
16.8.16 Henu	Nil	GK
17.8.16 "	Lines laid for Special Bde. Henu, Souastre RE +	GK
18.8.16 HENU	FONQUEVILLERS	GK
19.8.16 HENU	Linesman & Operators returned from SOUASTRE. SAILLY.AUX.BOIS. ST AMAND. 167 BDE 168 BDE. 169 BDE. Packing of Signal Stores.	GK

Gordon Kennard
Major RE
OC Signals 56 Division

INTELLIGENCE SUMMARY

(Erase heading not required.) 56 DIV Sig Co RE.

Instructions regarding War Diaries and Intelligence Summaries are contained in F.S. Regs., Part II. and the Staff Manual respectively. Title pages will be prepared in manuscript.

Hour, Date, Place	Summary of Events and Information	Remarks and references to Appendices
20/8/16 HENU	NIL	
21/8/16 HENU 9.30 AM	Company left by route march from HENU to DOULLENS with exception of 1 officer 3 NCO's 4 1 OR to clear + hand over to incomming Division	q.K.
22/8/16 DOULLENS 8.30 AM	Company left by route march from DOULLENS to FHROUN-LE-GRAND	q.K.
23/8/16 FHROUN-LE-GRAND	Company left by route march from FHROUN-LE-GRAND to St RIQUIER	q.K.
24/8/16 St RIQUIER	Laying lines from St RIQUIER to ARGEN VILLERS to CAPE NEWEST to IRUCAT E. Q. DUMPS etc	q.K.
25/8/16	As ABOVE 36 NCO's + MEN from Battalions reported for DIVISIONAL SIGNAL SCHOOL. Gordon Kennard major RE OC Signals 56 Division	q.K.

INTELLIGENCE SUMMARY

(Erase heading not required.) 56 Divisional Sig Coy RE

Hour, Date, Place	Summary of Events and Information	Remarks and references to Appendices
26/8/16 St RIQUIER	Training & Finishing LINES of Communication. 2 OR reported from BASE Signals	G.K.
27/8/16 "	Nil	G.K.
28/8/16 "	Conference of all Officers & Senior NCO's Engr Sigs in Signal work within the Division	G.K.
29/8/16 "	Training	G.K.
30/8/16 "	Training	G.K.
31/8/16 "	Training	G.K.

Gordon Kennard
Major RE.
OC Signals
56 Division

56th Divisional Engineers

56th DIVISIONAL SIGNAL COMPANY R. E.

SEPTEMBER 1916.

Army Form C. 2118.

WAR DIARY
or
INTELLIGENCE SUMMARY
(Erase heading not required.)

56 Divisional Signal Coy

Instructions regarding War Diaries and Intelligence Summaries are contained in F. S. Regs., Part II. and the Staff Manual respectively. Title pages will be prepared in manuscript.

Hour, Date, Place	Summary of Events and Information	Remarks and references to Appendices
St Riquier 1/9/16	Training	G.K.
St Riquier 2/9/16	"	G.K.
St Riquier 3/9/16 8.30 AM	Signal Company in charge of Lt H F Fox left by Route march for LONGPRE	
	HQ section remained in charge of office at ST RIQUIER	G.K.
CORBIE 4/9/16 10.30 AM	Established Div HQ Sig office at CORBIE	G.K.
LONGPRE 8.30 AM	Signal Coy left LONGPRE by route march for CORBIE arriving 3.30 PM	G.K.
CORBIE 9.30 AM 5/9/16	Signal Coy left CORBIE by route march for FORK TREE on BRAY - MEAULT RD arriving 4 PM	G.K.
FORK TREE 6/9/16	Signal Coy moved to BILLONS FARM.	G.K. Gordon Kennard Major R.E.

Army Form C. 2118.

WAR DIARY
or
INTELLIGENCE SUMMARY

(Erase heading not required.)

56 Divisional Signal Coy RE

Hour, Date, Place	Summary of Events and Information	Remarks and references to Appendices
7/9/16 BILLONS FARM	Signal Coy laying lines for Communications for operations. Ref 56 Div Order No 33 attached.	gk
8/9/16 BILLONS FARM	2Lt ARTHUR replaced 2nd Lieut GYRON at 167 BDE SECTION. Through Sickness	gk.
9/9/16 BILLONS FARM	Attack of the 56 Division on the German line Diagram of Communications to Bdes concerned 169 Bde on the right 168 Bde on the left overleaf	gk.

Gordon Kennard
Major RE
O C Signals 56 Division

Army Form C. 2118.

WAR DIARY
or
INTELLIGENCE SUMMARY

(Erase heading not required.)

56 Divisional Signal Coy

Instructions regarding War Diaries and Intelligence Summaries are contained in F. S. Regs., Part II. and the Staff Manual respectively. Title pages will be prepared in manuscript.

Hour, Date, Place	Summary of Events and Information	Remarks and references to Appendices
10/9/16 BILLONS FARM	Operations continued. 2nd Lieut COLEMAN.F.W. reported for duty from England	G.K.
11/9/16 BILLONS FARM	2nd Lieut PARKINSON.W reported for duty from XIV CORPS	G.K.
12/9/16 BILLONS FARM	2nd LIEUT YALE H.E.T. reported for duty from XIV Corps. Signal Coy on Lines of Communication for fresh operations Vide Divisional Order No 36 Copy No 16 attached	G.K.

Gordon Kennard
Major RE
O C Signals 56 Div

1247 W 3299 200,000 (E) 8/14 J.B.C. & A. Forms/C. 2118/11.

Army Form C. 2118.

WAR DIARY
or
INTELLIGENCE SUMMARY

(Erase heading not required.)

Instructions regarding War Diaries and Intelligence Summaries are contained in F. S. Regs., Part II. and the Staff Manual respectively. Title pages will be prepared in manuscript.

Hour, Date, Place	Summary of Events and Information	Remarks and references to Appendices
13/9/16 Billons Farm	Continuation of work Communications established vide Divisional Order No 37 Copy No 16 (to be attached) Diagram overleaf Signalling instructions for operations attached Copy of Visual instructions attached	G.K. G.K. Gordon Kennard Major R.E. O.C. Signals 5 6 Division

Army Form C. 2118.

WAR DIARY
or
INTELLIGENCE SUMMARY
(Erase heading not required.)

Instructions regarding War Diaries and Intelligence Summaries are contained in F. S. Regs., Part II. and the Staff Manual respectively. Title pages will be prepared in manuscript.

56 Division C in C R.E.

Hour, Date, Place	Summary of Events and Information	Remarks and references to Appendices
14/9/16 Billons Farm	Laying Lines for opperations. Divisional Headquarters moved to A10 & 65 Boles to FALFEMONT FARM. ANGLE 11000 & CRUCIFIX. HARDECOURT.	G.K.
15/9/16	Following NCO & OR Wounded Sapper Davis Sap Capp Sapper Hunt Sap Norris Sapper Quarrington Driver Smith Sapper Roberts	G.K.
15/9/16	Opperations commenced	G.K. Gordon Kennard Major R.E. O C Signals 56 Div.

Army Form C. 2118.

WAR DIARY
or
INTELLIGENCE SUMMARY

(Erase heading not required.)

56 Divisional Signal Coy RE

Hour, Date, Place	Summary of Events and Information	Remarks and references to Appendices
16.9.16 GERMAN TRENCH	Operations continued. L/Corp HALL N. wounded	G.K.
17.9.16 GERMAN TRENCH	Operations continued	G.K.
18.9.16 German TRENCH	Operations continued	G.K.
19.9.16 GERMAN TRENCH	Operations continued	G.K.
20.9.16 GERMAN TRENCH	Operations continued	G.K.
21.9.16 GERMAN TRENCH	Divn H.Q. moved from GERMAN TRENCH TO BILLON FARM. Operations continued	G.K. G.K.
	Following O.R. from SIGNAL DEPOT KNIGHTS, A. ALLEN C.T. SIMPSON GARDNER SILVERS ELSDON	G.K. G. Kennard Major, RE O C Sigs 56 Divn

1247 W 3299 200,000 (E) 8/14 J.B.C. & A. Forms/C. 2118/11.

Army Form C. 2118.

WAR DIARY
or
INTELLIGENCE SUMMARY

(Erase heading not required.)

56th Divisional Signal Coy R.E.

Instructions regarding War Diaries and Intelligence Summaries are contained in F.S. Regs., Part II. and the Staff Manual respectively. Title pages will be prepared in manuscript.

Hour, Date, Place	Summary of Events and Information	Remarks and references to Appendices
22.9.16 Billon Farm	Operations continued	G.K.
23.9.16 Billon Farm	A/L/c VAUGHAN J.H. 225-3 reported for duty. Operations continued. for vanguard	G.K.
24.9.16 Billon Farm	1 OR WOUNDED OPERATIONS CONTINUED Sap HARDING GH 1607	G.K.
25.9.16 Billon Farm	FURTHER ADVANCE. 2101 Sap MITTEN BA KILLED in action	G.K.
26.9.16 Billon Farm	OPERATIONS CONTINUED	G.K.
27.9.16 Billon Farm	"	G.K.
28.9.16 Billon Farm	168 BDE Relieved by French.	G.K.
29.9.16 Billon Farm	SITUATION Normal	G.K.
30th 9.16 10AM GERMAN TRENCH	2nd LIEUT D.W. ALDRIGE reported for duty. SIGNAL Coys moved to GERMAN TRENCH lines Laid to BDES DIAGRAM of event as over.	G.K. Gordon Kennard major RE

Army Form C. 2118.

WAR DIARY
or
INTELLIGENCE SUMMARY

(Erase heading not required.)

Instructions regarding War Diaries and Intelligence Summaries are contained in F. S. Regs., Part II. and the Staff Manual respectively. Title pages will be prepared in manuscript.

Hour, Date, Place	Summary of Events and Information	Remarks and references to Appendices

COMMUNICATIONS OF Y.E.F.

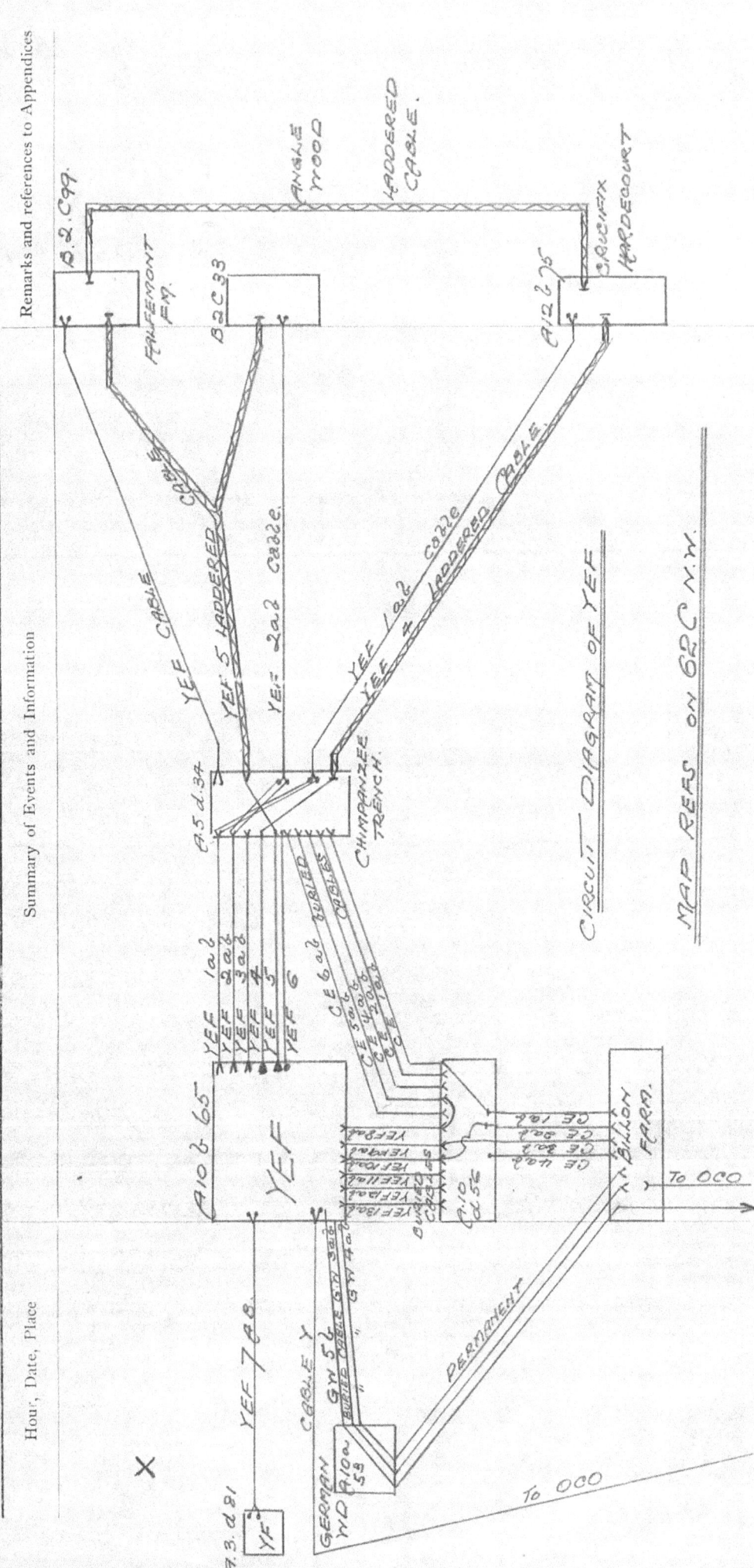

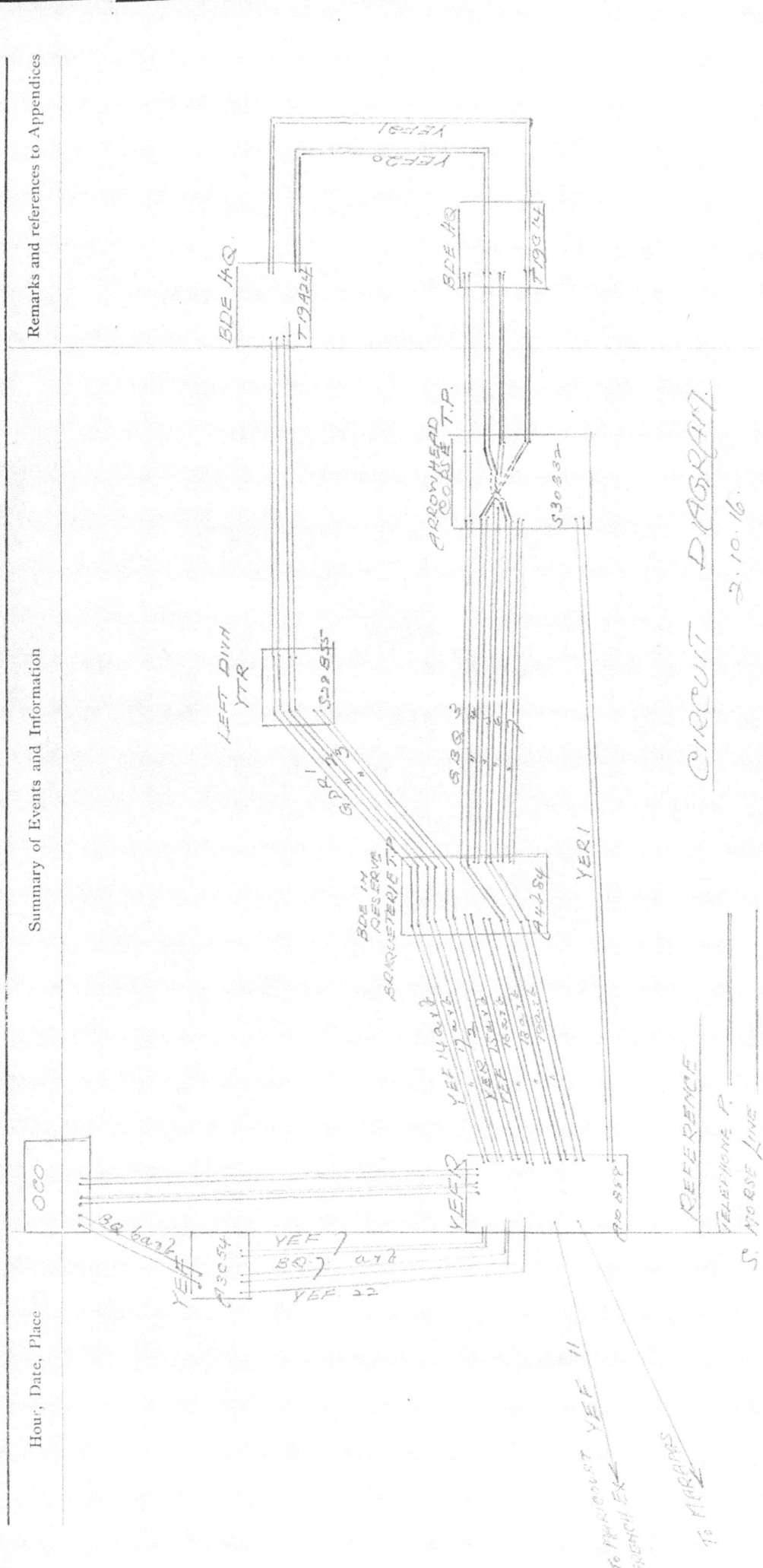

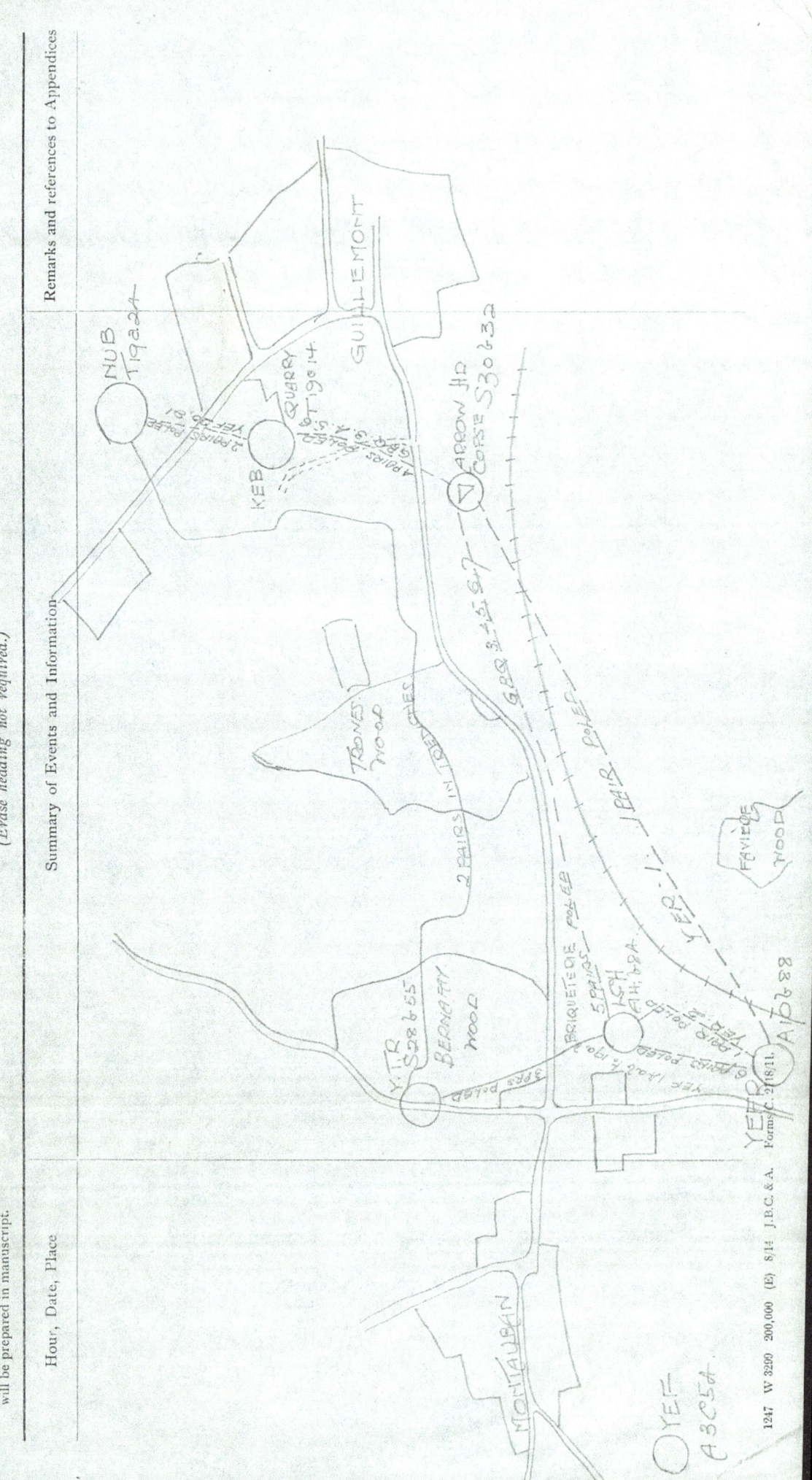

SECRET.

56th DIVISIONAL ORDER No. 33.

7th September, 1916.

1. The XIVth Corps is renewing the attack on the 9th September in conjunction with Corps to the North.

2. The objective of the 56th Division is the German position from T.27.b.1.5½. - T.21.d.5½.2½. Point 141.7 (1,000 yards East of GINCHY).

The objective of the 16th Division is the trench along the GINCHY - MORVAL road to trench junction T.14.c.5.4½ - T.14.a.4.2., thence to junction of trenches at T.7.d.4.0.

3. The dividing line between divisions will be a line from the GUILLEMONT - LEUZE WOOD ROAD at T.20.d.1.5. to trench junction at T.14.d.8½.4. (inclusive to 56th Division).

The attack of the 56th Division will be carried out by the 169th Infantry Brigade on the right and the 168th Infantry Brigade on the left.

4. The dividing line between Brigades will be the road running N.N.E. from the N. Corner of LEUZE WOOD to the point where the trench crosses the road in T.21.a.

5. (a) The objective of 169th Infantry Brigade is the German trench T.27.b.1.5½. - T.21.d.5½.2½. - T.21.a.8.2½.

(b). The first objective of 168th Infantry Brigade, road from the N. Corner of LEUZE WOOD to T.20.b.4.3., including the capture of the German trench from T.20.d.2.9. to T.20.b.9.1.

(c). The 2nd objective of the 168th Infantry Brigade is the German trench from T.21.a.6.2½. - T.15.c.1.4½. - T.14.d.8½.4.

6. (a). The attack will be preceded by a bombardment of heavy artillery, details of which will be published separately by the General Officer Commanding, R.A., XIVth Corps.

During the bombardment certain trenches may have to be cleared from time to time.

(b). Fifty per cent of the Field Artillery guns covering each Division will be employed for a stationary barrage, and fifty per cent for a creeping barrage.

/ The.

Visual Instructions.

Observation Station at CRUCIFIX should remain open particularly observing - and observe Signals from 126, & 95. LEUZE WOOD.

1. An Officer attached from Corps Signals Lt Vale will supervise this Station in Conjunction with the Bde Signalling Officer of the 169th Bde.

2. A French Signalling lamp has been delivered to the Signalling Sergeant. Q.V.R.s & further lamps have been sent to 169 & 168th Bdes, no further lamps or discs are available from Corps, so Bde Signalling Officers must make arrangements to recall one of those lamps already issued to their Battalion also discs.

SECRET.   Copy No. 16

56th DIVISIONAL ORDER No. 36.
                                                    12th September, 1916.

1. The relief of a portion of the 167th Infantry Brigade (as outlined in 56th Divisional Order No. 35) by the 16th Infantry Brigade will be completed tonight.

2. The Composite Infantry Brigade of 5th Division holding the Right Sector of the 56th Divisional front will be relieved by troops of the 56th Division on night 13th/14th September, as follows:-

   (a). 167th Infantry Brigade will take over the Divisional front North of point T.27.a.2.4. Southern Corner of LEUZE WOOD.
   (b). 169th Infantry Brigade will take over the Divisional front South of point T.27.a.2.4.

3. The distribution of troops will be arranged as follows:-

   Right Brigade
     2 Battalions   - Forward area including front line and trenches about FALFEMONT FARM and ANGLE WOOD.
     1 Battalion   - About A.12.b.
     1 Battalion   - About A.10.c.
     Brigade H.Q.   - At CRUCIFIX A.12.b.9.2.

   Left Brigade
     2 Battalions   - Forward area including front line and trenches about WEDGE WOOD.
     1 Battalion   - About A.12.a.
     1 Battalion   - About A.10.a.
     Brigade H.Q.   - H.Q. now occupied by 13th Inf. Bde. at A.5.d.3.3.

4. Details regarding relief will be carried out by Brigadiers concerned direct.

5. Under no circumstances will any troops of the 13th Infantry Brigade be withdrawn until they have been properly relieved and the commander of the relieving unit is satisfied as to the situation.

   -On relief-
6. Composite Infantry Brigade, less two battalions of the 95th Brigade will move to MERICOURT. The two battalions of the 95th Brigade will proceed to VILLE-SUR-ANCRE. Bivouac ground now occupied by 169th Infantry Brigade near BILLON FARM is available to halt in, but must be clear of troops by 11.0 am. 13th inst. Troops will move to MERICOURT, via FILIFORM TREE and cross country tracks - VILLE-SUR-ANCRE - TREUX.

7. 138th Infantry Brigade will remain in their present bivouac near BILLON FARM.

8. ACKNOWLEDGE.

Hdqrs. 56th Divn.
                                        A.H. Bayley Major
12th September, 1916.   for Lieut. Colonel,
                                        General Staff.

           Issued at 12.30 pm. 12.9.16.
Copy Nos:-
  1. XIVth Corps "G".   7. 138th Inf.Bde.   13.)French Liaison
  2. XIVth Corps "Q".   8. 169th "   "   14.)   Officer.
  3. G.O.C. 56th Div.   9. A.D.M.S.   15. 5th Ches. Regt.
  4. 5th Divn.   10. C.R.E.   16. Signals.
  5. Composite Bde.5th Div. 11. C.R.A.   17. 6th Division.
  6. 167th Inf. Bde.   12. "Q".   18. 1st Cav. Divn.

SIGNALLING INSTRUCTIONS.

Issued in connection with 56th Divisional Order No.37.

1. **VISUAL.** The following visual signalling posts will be established for the forthcoming operations. These posts will each consist of 1 N.C.O. and 4 men, which will be detailed by Brigades as mentioned in table below.

    The men should be specially selected Battalion Signallers, as the personnel of the Divisional Signal Company is not sufficient to meet the demand.

    The men selected should report to Officers in charge of Brigade Signal Section by 2.0 p.m. 14th instant.

    Lamps and discs will be provided by the O.C. Divisional Signal Company. Instructions as to the siting of these signal posts will be issued by O.C. Divisional Signal Co. to Officers in charge of Brigade Signal Section.

Brigade finding personnel.	Position of Post about	Remarks.
167th Inf.Bde.	T.29.b.9.5.	Communicate with CRUCIFIX.
167th Inf.Bde.	B.2.d.3.0.	Communicate with CRUCIFIX and observe LEUZE WOOD.
168th Inf.Bde.	B.2.c.1.5.	Communicate with CRUCIFIX and observe FALFEMONT FARM.
169th Inf. Bde.	CRUCIFIX	Observe all forward Stations.

2. **TELEGRAPHS.** Direct laddered lines have been established between the Divisional Report Centre at A.10.b.5.5. and each of the 3 Brigade H.Q.
    Laddered lines have also been established between 167th and 169th Infantry Brigade H.Q. giving an alternate route for telegraph work.

3. **TELEPHONES.** A pair of telephone lines (metallic circuit) have been laid to each Brigade H.Q., to the 5th Division on our right, and 2nd French Division on our left, and to the Cavalry Div. H.Q. at A.5.d.5.4.

4. **WIRELESS.** A wireless set has been installed at the CRUCIFIX N. of HARDECOURT, and the second set will be installed near 167th Infantry Brigade H.Q. by FALFEMONT FARM.

5. **PIGEONS.** 9 Pigeons will be delivered to 167th and 168th Inf. Bdes.
    Attention should be called to the fact that messages requiring instant action such as an "S.O.S." should not be sent by pigeon service, as it takes about one hour for messages to get through by which time the local conditions may probably have completely altered.

Situation

Situation reports or demands for special stores to be sent up, etc., might very usefully be sent by pigeon service when other means of communication fail.

Birds should not be "pitched" within one hour of darkness as birds will not "Home" till the following day.

[signature]

Hdqrs. 56th Divn.
14th September, 1916.

Lieut. Colonel,
General Staff

Signal Coy
4th N.M.

To Headquarters
56th Division

Herewith War Diary for
the month of October

G. Carpenter
for Major R.E.
O.C. Signals
56th Division

56th DIVISIONAL
SIGNAL COMPANY
R.E.
No. R 840
Date 2.11.16

Passed to you

Army Form C. 2118.

WAR DIARY
or
INTELLIGENCE SUMMARY   56 Divisional Signal Coy R.E.

(Erase heading not required.)

Instructions regarding War Diaries and Intelligence Summaries are contained in F. S. Regs., Part II. and the Staff Manual respectively. Title pages will be prepared in manuscript.

Hour, Date, Place	Summary of Events and Information	Remarks and references to Appendices
October 1 GERMAN WD	Operations continued	G.K.
Oct 2 GERMAN WD	" Divisional Signalling " taken over lines of communication of 4th Division before taking over	
Oct 3 GERMAN WD	168 Bde relieved 169 Bde Section	G.K.
Oct 4 GERMAN WD	Operations continued. A working party provided for burying cables on XIV Corps Route to Front line.	G.K. G.K.
Oct 5 GERMAN WD	Operations continued Lt H Barker returned from Hospital & took charge of 169 Bde communications	G.K.
Oct 6 GERMAN WD	Conference at XIV Corps of Div Sig officers	G.K.
	Gordon Kennard Major RE O C Signals 56 Div	

WAR DIARY or INTELLIGENCE SUMMARY

Army Form C. 2118.

56 Divisional Signal Co^y s

Hour, Date, Place	Summary of Events and Information	Remarks and references to Appendices
Oct 7. 1916 GERMAN WD	attack on Brown LINE W of LE TRANSLOY	QK
Oct 8th 1916 GERMAN WD	Operations continued 8 O R under Lt QE Carpenter proceeded to Rest Camp 2nd Lt E. Williams took over 168 BDE Communications	
	1 O R 152602 Cpl NORMAN A R from Signal Depot reported for duty	QK
Oct 9th GERMAN WD	Relief of Signal sections 167, 168 169 Bde completed by Signal Sections 10. 11 + 12 Bdes	QK QK
	1 O R 90806 Driver FREEMAN H from Signal Depot reported for duty	QK
Oct 10th GERMAN WD	Divisional Signal Co^{ys} proceeded to Citadel HQ established 10 AM 2 sections despatched to establish HQ at BELLOY SUR SOMME. Kenmuir major OC Signals 56 Div	QK QK

Army Form C. 2118.

WAR DIARY
or
INTELLIGENCE SUMMARY
(Erase heading not required.)

56 Divisional Signal Coy

Hour, Date, Place	Summary of Events and Information	Remarks and references to Appendices
11 Oct 1914 CITADEL	Div Signal Coy proceeded by ROUTE MARCH to CORBIE arriving 5 PM	C.K.
12 Oct 1914 CORBIE	LEFT CORBIE at 8.30 AM by ROUTE MARCH for BELLOY SUR SOMME arriving 7.30 PM	C.K.
13 Oct BELLOY SUR SOMME	Communications established to Corps 167, 168, 169 Bdes & H F FOX returned from Hospital	C.K.
14 Oct Belloy sur Somme	Rgt No 2364 J Roos (under age) departed for Base Company resting.	C.K.
15 Oct Belloy SUR SOMME	Rgt No 171845 Pn BALBIRNIE A E & 3362 SAPPER HARVEY W F G reported for duty from Signal Depot G Kennard Major RE OC Signals 56 Division	C.K.

Army Form C. 2118.

WAR DIARY
or
INTELLIGENCE SUMMARY
(Erase heading not required.)

5-6 Divisional Signal Coy

Instructions regarding War Diaries and Intelligence Summaries are contained in F. S. Regs., Part II. and the Staff Manual respectively. Title pages will be prepared in manuscript.

Hour, Date, Place	Summary of Events and Information	Remarks and references to Appendices
16 Oct BELLOY SUR SOMME.	Court-Martial of 2nd LIEUT F W COLEMAN. 2002 Cpl H A Johnson departed for Flying Corps on one months probation	G K
17 Oct Belloy sur Somme	Company parades as usual	G K
18 Oct BELLOY SOR SOMME	" " "	G K
19 Oct 1916 BELLOY sur SOMME	advance party consisting of 1 section left for HALLENCOURT to establish Communication	G K
	LT H F FOX + 2nd LT MASLIN H¹ departed on special leave	G K
20th Oct BELLOY sur SOMME	Divisional Signal Co"s proceeded by ROUTE MARCH for HALLENCOURT arriving at 8PM	G K
	G Kennard Major RE OC Signals 56 Div	G K

1247 W 3299 200,000 (E) 8/14 J.M.G.& A. Forms/C. 2118/11.

Army Form C. 2118.

WAR DIARY
or
INTELLIGENCE SUMMARY

(Erase heading not required.)

56 Divisional Signal Cos R E

Hour, Date, Place	Summary of Events and Information	Remarks and references to Appendices
21 Oct HALLENCOURT	Communication established to Coys 167. 168. 169 Bde	qk
22 Oct HALLENCOURT	Advance parties of 2 sections left to establish communications at LESTREM. 1604 Qu M Cockburn 12975! Sapr W Eyre 12'75.80 Pr W Puckenfield reported from Signal Depot	qk
23 Oct HALLENCOURT	Company left by route march to entrain at LONG-PRE	qk
24 Oct 1916 LONG-PRE	Divisional Signal Cos entrained LESTREM 6 PM	qk qk L Kennard Major RE OC Signals 56 Div

Army Form C. 2118.

WAR DIARY
or
INTELLIGENCE SUMMARY
(Erase heading not required.)

56 Divisional Signal Coy R E

Hour, Date, Place	Summary of Events and Information	Remarks and references to Appendices
25 Oct 1916 LESTREM	Communications established 167, 168,169 Brest Corps	OK
26 Oct 1916 LESTREM	RESTING	OK
27 Oct 1916 LESTREM	Advance party left proceeded to Division in the LINE HQ at LE GORGUE	OK
28 Oct 1916 LESTREM	Divisional Signal Coy proceed by Route march for LE GORGUE Took Over LINES of Communications from 61st Division all OK at 4.30 PM	OK
29 Oct 1916 LE GORGUE	Situation Normal	OK

E Kennard
Major RE
OC Signals 56 Division

Army Form C. 2118.

WAR DIARY
or
INTELLIGENCE SUMMARY

(Erase heading not required.)

56 Divisional Signal Coys RE

Hour, Date, Place	Summary of Events and Information	Remarks and references to Appendices
30th Oct LA GORGUE	2nd Lt F W Coleman returned to England 1st H Barber proceeded on Special Leave 2/Lt E Williams took over communications of 168 Bde 898 Driver Hunter RE 2581 Driver Sersons S 23631 Driver Hotkins y 3216 Pn St Aimes AC reported from Signal Depot Situation normal.	GK GK GK GK GK
31st Oct LA GORGUE	2/Lt Q E Carpenter reported from 168 BDE for duty 2nd in Command Situation normal	GK GK

Gordon Kennard
Major RE
OC Signals 56 Division

Army Form C. 2118.

WAR DIARY
or
INTELLIGENCE SUMMARY

(Erase heading not required.)

55th DIVISIONAL SIGNAL COMPANY R.E.

No. A. 1088.
Date 2.12.16.

Hour, Date, Place		Summary of Events and Information	Remarks and references to Appendices
1st Nov.	La GORGUE.	Situation normal.	H.P.C.
2nd Nov.	"	1 Sgt. 9 O.R. reported from 15th Cheshire Regt. for temporary duty. 2/Lt. C.W. ARTHUR reported from hospital.	do.
3rd "	"	Situation normal.	do.
4th "	"	Situation normal.	do.
5th "	"	2 offrs. 12 O.R. reported from 55th Divnl. Cas. Regt. for duty. 2/Lt. H.I. MASLIN and Lt. F.H. FOX rejoined unit from leave. Lt. F.H. FOX reported for duty to 167th Inf. Bde. Sig. 127756 SAP. CHAPMAN A. 3269 PNR BRADFORD H. reinforcement from Signal Depot.	do.
6th "	"	1 offr 12 OR left for duty with 55th Div. ARTY.	do.
7th "	"	Situation normal.	do.
8th "	"	do. do.	do.
9th "	"	do. do.	do.
10th "	"	1 offr 7 OR reported from Corps for duty - as Area Maintenance Pty. 1658 SGT. HILDER C.J. left for 1st Army Sig. School as instructor.	do.
11th "	"	Lt. H. BARBER rejoined unit from leave. Conference of Signal Officers of units of 55th Division.	do.
12th "	"	60 O.R. from battalions reported for Divnl. Sig. School. Lt. H. BARBER left for 1st Army Sig. School as instructor.	do.

Army Form C. 2118.

WAR DIARY
or
INTELLIGENCE SUMMARY

(Erase heading not required.)

Instructions regarding War Diaries and Intelligence Summaries are contained in F. S. Regs., Part II. and the Staff Manual respectively. Title pages will be prepared in manuscript.

Hour, Date, Place		Summary of Events and Information	Remarks and references to Appendices
13TH NOV.	LA GORGUE.	Divisional Signal School opened. Situation normal.	JR
14TH	"	Situation normal.	
15TH	"	Distribution of medal ribbons to SGT E. DEATH 1641. A/SGT DALTRY. R. 986 by O/Pr Commander. Situation normal.	JR
16TH	"	Situation normal.	JR
17TH	"	do	JR
18TH	"	Cmdg. Offr attended Conference of Sig. Offrs at Corps Hqrs. 2/Lt C.F. CLARK reported for duty from 3/1st LOND DIVNL SIG. Co.	JR
19TH	"	Situation normal	JR
20TH	"	3195 Pte ARMOUR A.E. 77,048 Dr PASSINGHAM F. 17826. Dr CREE J. reinforcements from Signal Depot.	JR
21ST	"	Situation normal.	JR
22ND	"	Major G. KENNARD proceedd on leave. Capt G.E. CARPENTER assumed Command of 5th Divnl Sig. Co.	JR
23RD	"	Situation normal.	JR
24TH	"	Situation normal.	JR
25TH	"	2/LT SW ARTHUR Transferred to 5th Divnl Sig. Co. 2/Lt E. WILLIAM to hospital. Situation normal.	JR
26TH	"	2/Lt C.F. CLARK reported to 14th Inf BDE for duty as Bde. Sig. offr.	JR
27TH	"	All conversation prohibited for 24 hrs. over lines in "forward" area.	JR
		3117 Sap SAUNDERS G. 21342. Dr LONG. T. reinforcement from Signal Depot	JR

1247 W 3299 200,000 (E) 8/14 J.B.C. & A. Forms/C. 2118/11.

Army Form C. 2118.

WAR DIARY
or
INTELLIGENCE SUMMARY

(Erase heading not required.)

Instructions regarding War Diaries and Intelligence Summaries are contained in F. S. Regs., Part II, and the Staff Manual respectively. Title pages will be prepared in manuscript.

Hour, Date, Place	Summary of Events and Information	Remarks and references to Appendices
28th Nov. La Gorgue	Situation Normal.	
29th " "	2/Lt H.I. Marsuit reports to Central Wireless School, G.H.Q. for Technical Course.	
30th " "	Lt H.E.T. Vale, A.S.I. Granted Leave. Situation Normal.	

G.A. Stewart Capt RE
O/C Signal. 36th. Division.

53rd DIVISIONAL
SIGNAL COMPANY.
R.E.

Army Form C. 2118.

56 Divisional Signal Coy RE

WAR DIARY
or
INTELLIGENCE SUMMARY

(Erase heading not required.)

Hour, Date, Place		Summary of Events and Information	Remarks and references to Appendices
Dec 1	La Gorgue	Situation normal.	RLO
" 2	"	Situation normal	RLO
" 3	"	2650 Dr Jones. J.M. 3301 Sap. Geary.J. reported from Signal depot.	RLO
" 4	"	Situation normal	RLO
" 5	"	Ser/Lt H.I. Maslin reported to unit from Central Wireless School. G.H.Q.	RLO
" 6	"	56th Div. Arty Sig Took over from 6th Divl Arty Sigs.	RLO
" 7	"	Situation normal.	RLO
" 8	"	Situation normal	GK
" 9	"	Lt H E T Vale returned from leave	GK
" 10	"	Divisional Signal School terminates Battalion signallers return to their units	GK
" 11	"	D.D.A.S. visited area	GK
" 12	"	Situation normal	GK

Gordon Kennard
Major RE
OC Signal 56 Div

Army Form C. 2118.

WAR DIARY
or
INTELLIGENCE SUMMARY
(Erase heading not required.)

56 Divisional Signal Coy RE

Hour, Date, Place	Summary of Events and Information	Remarks and references to Appendices
13.12.1916 La Gourge	Situation normal	GK
14 " "	Lt F B Finter reported for duty	GK
15 " "	Situation normal	GK
16 " "	Situation normal	GK
17 " La Gourge	Battalion signallers report for the 6th Divisional School (60)	GK
18 " "	Signalling School opens	GK
19 " "	Situation normal	GK
20 " "	Situation normal	GK
21 " "	Situation normal	GK
22 " "	Situation normal	GK
23 " "	Situation normal	GK
24 " La Gourge	2nd CF Clerk to Army Wireless School	GK
25.12 La Gourge	182008 Sap Hill BJ 194695 Sapper Peckham 77129 Sapper Daplyn WC 194894 Sapper Drow G reinforcements from Signal Depot	GK

Gordon Kennard
Major RE OC Signals
56 Division

Army Form C. 2118.

WAR DIARY
or
INTELLIGENCE SUMMARY

(Erase heading not required.)

5-6 Divisional Signal Coy R.E.(T)

Instructions regarding War Diaries and Intelligence Summaries are contained in F. S. Regs., Part II. and the Staff Manual respectively. Title pages will be prepared in manuscript.

Hour, Date, Place	Summary of Events and Information	Remarks and references to Appendices
26.12.16 LA COURVE	Situation normal	G.K.
27.12.16 "	Situation normal	G.K.
28.12.16 LA COURVE	Situation normal	G.K.
29.12.16 "	Situation normal	G.K.
30.12.16 LA COURVE	Situation normal	G.K.
31.12.16 LA COURVE	2 Lt F C Clark returned from Army Wireless Course	

Gordon Kennard
Major R.E.(T)
O.C. Signals
56 Division

To Headquarters
56th Div.

Herewith War Diary for January 1917

Gordon Kennard.
Major R.E.
OC Signals
56th Divn

Army Form C. 2118.

WAR DIARY
or
INTELLIGENCE SUMMARY
(Erase heading not required.)

56 Div Signal Coy RE (TF)

Hour, Date, Place	Summary of Events and Information	Remarks and references to Appendices
1st Jan 1917 LR COURCELLE	3 officers mentioned in despatches. HQ section. 2LTH Barber No 2 section 2nd LT H.I. MASLIN No 4 Section.	G.K.
2nd Jan 1917 "	A.F.B FINTER Left for CANADIAN CORPS SIGNAL Co's	G.K.
3rd " 1917 "	PB Cable Section arrived from Corps EO as rest. 157 BDE SIGNALS	G.K. G.K.
	2LT H BARBER transferred to 1st ARMY Signals	G.K.
4th " 1917 "	Situation normal	G.K.
5th " 1917 "	Situation normal	G.K.
	Laid Cables in new 6FT TRENCH at LEFT BDE HQ & completed	G.K. G.K.
6th " 1917 "	SITUATION NORMAL Relaying GLD ROUTE Ans 6+6	G.K.
7th " 1917 "	2ND LIEUT H.F. BALL L.R.B & 2nd LIEUT F.J. BECK QWR Battalion Signalling officers reported for duty 16 days refresher course with Divisional Signals	G.K. G.K.
8th " 1917 "	Packing up old derelict lines along Railway. 1066 Corp A.S. EVANS 2853 Corp J.F ALDRICH 165418 Pioneer HOLTZ PN reinforcements reported from Signal Depot. Situation normal	G.K. G.K. G.K.
9th " 1917 "	Reconstruction of CP ROUTE commenced	G.K.

Gordon Kenward
O.C. Signals 56 Division

Army Form C. 2118.

WAR DIARY
or
INTELLIGENCE SUMMARY
(Erase heading not required.)

56 Div Signal Coy RE (TF)

Place	Date	Hour	Summary of Events and Information	Remarks and references to Appendices
LA ROOREVE	10.1.17		Situation NORMAL.	G.K.
"	11.1.17		2nd LT N ALDRIDGE departed to Corps for Aeroplane Course. Situation Normal	G.K.
"	12.1.17		Renewing the R.L & C.P. routes (Telegraph)	G.K.
"	13.1.17		Situation normal. work continued	G.K.
"	14.1.17		5th Divisional Signal School terminates. 60 Battalion & artillery Signallers returned to their units	G.K.
"	15.1.17		2nd LIEUT H.F. Ball detailed to 169 Bde Signals for instruction. Many alterations at (Boek SKY HOUSE = Post Office LEVENT) commenced G/k	G.K.
"	16.1.17		2nd LT N WALDRIGH returned from Corps	G.K.
"	19.1.17		Situation normal	G.K.
"	18.1.17		2nd LT N WALDRIGE departed on leave. Test Dugouts commenced at Left Bde.	G.K.
"	19.1.17		Situation normal.	G.K.
"	20.1.17		NEW AIR LINE EXTENSIONS at Bde HQ commenced	G.K.
"	21.1.17		6th Divisional Signal School for Artillery (6.O.O.R) Report.	G.K.

Gordon Kennard
Major RE
OC Signals 56 Div

Army Form C. 2118.

WAR DIARY
or
INTELLIGENCE SUMMARY

(Erase heading not required.)

56 Divisional Signal Coy RE

Place	Date	Hour	Summary of Events and Information	Remarks and references to Appendices
LA COURCE	22.1.17		2nd Lieut W Parkinson departed for Wadffen course GHQ.	GK
"			165873 Pioneer W Perry reinforcement from Signal Depot	GK
"			60 Artillery Regraters report for Signal School.	GK
	23.1.17		Situation normal.	
"	24.1.17		Attended conference & Lecture of Divisional Signals at gunner Staff College GHQ	GK
"	25.1.17		Situation normal	GK
"	26.1.17		Situation normal	GK
"	27.1.17		Situation normal	GK
"	28.1.17		Situation normal	GK
"	29.1.17		2/Lt W Parkinson returned from GHQ Wireless course Situation normal	GK
"	30.1.17		Situation normal	GK
"	31.1.17		Situation normal	GK

Gordon Kennard
Major RE
OC Signals 56 Division

Army Form C. 2118.

WAR DIARY
or
INTELLIGENCE SUMMARY
(Erase heading not required.)

56 Div Signal Cos R E (T F)

Instructions regarding War Diaries and Intelligence Summaries are contained in F. S. Regs., Part II. and the Staff Manual respectively. Title pages will be prepared in manuscript.

Hour, Date, Place | Summary of Events and Information | Remarks and references to Appendices

Gordon Kennard
Major R.E.T.
O C Signals 56 H(?)

To Headquarters
56th Divn

Herewith War Diary for month of February 1917.

G C Carpenter
Capt. RE
OC Sigs
56th Divn

56th DIVISIONAL
SIGNAL COMPANY
R.E.
No. C 881
Date 1.3.17

Army Form C. 2118.

WAR DIARY
or
INTELLIGENCE SUMMARY

56 D Signals

JM/3

(Erase heading not required.)

Instructions regarding War Diaries and Intelligence Summaries are contained in F. S. Regs., Part II. and the Staff Manual respectively. Title Pages will be prepared in manuscript.

Place	Date	Hour	Summary of Events and Information	Remarks and references to Appendices
La Gorgue	1.2.1917	—	227 D.W. ALDRIDGE reported from leave	AO
"	2.2.1917	—	Divisional front extended to right. Communication established to Sub.H.Qrs at HUITS-MAISONS.	AO
"	3.2.1917	—	Situation normal.	AO
"	4.2.1917	—	Capt G.E. CARPENTER (actg) 11 days leave.	AO
"	5.2.1917	—	Situation normal	AO
"	6.2.1917	—	Situation normal	AO
"	7.2.1917	—	Situation normal	AO
"	8.2.1917	—	Situation normal	AO
"	9.2.1917	—	Situation normal	AO
"	10.2.1917	—	1856 Sap. Fletcher A.H.G. 34781 Sap. Allen A.G reported as reinforcements from Signal Depot.	AO
"	11.2.1917	—	Situation normal	AO
"	12.2.1917	—	Situation normal	AO
"	13.2.1917	—	Situation normal	AO
"	14.2.1917	—	Test dug-out completed at "Post Office" Buried Cable Trench, Laventie.	AO
"	15.2.1917	—	Situation normal	AO

Army Form C. 2118.

WAR DIARY
or
INTELLIGENCE SUMMARY
(Erase heading not required.)

Instructions regarding War Diaries and Intelligence Summaries are contained in F.S. Regs., Part II. and the Staff Manual respectively. Title Pages will be prepared in manuscript.

Place	Date	Hour	Summary of Events and Information	Remarks and references to Appendices
La Gorgue	16.2.1917	—	Station normal.	
"	17.2.1917	—	CAPT. G.E. CARPENTER reported from leave.	
"	18.2.1917	—	Buried cable system at GORGHY HO, LAVENTIE. Completed.	
"	19.2.1917	—	MAJOR G. KENNARD evacuated to C.C.S.	
"	20.2.1917	—	New air-line route completed between GORGHY HO. LAVENTIE and HUITES - MATSONS.	
"	21.2.1917		Station normal.	
"	22.2.1917		Station normal.	
"	23.2.1917		2ᴺᴰ Lt. J.V.R. RAYNER reported for duty from 1ˢᵀ ARMY SIG Cᴼ.	
"	24.2.1917		Station normal.	
"	25.2.1917		Station normal.	
"	26.2.1917		Station normal.	
"	27.2.1917		Divisional front extended. Communications established to new area.	
"	28.2.1917		Station normal.	

(Signed) .... Capt. R.E.(T)
5ᵗʰ Divᴸ Sig Cᴼ

2449 Wt. W14957/Mg0 750,000 1/16 J.B.C. & A. Forms/C.2118/12.

To Headquarters
56 Divn

Herewith War Diary
for month of March, 1917.

[signature]
Capt. R.E.
i/c Sigs.
56 Divn

56th DIVISIONAL
SIGNAL COMPANY
R. E.
No. C.2027
Date 1.4.17.

Army Form C. 2118.

56 R__ Signal Co
Vol. 14

WAR DIARY
or
INTELLIGENCE SUMMARY.
(Erase heading not required.)

Instructions regarding War Diaries and Intelligence Summaries are contained in F. S. Regs., Part II and the Staff Manual respectively. Title pages will be prepared in manuscript.

Place	Date	Hour	Summary of Events and Information	Remarks and references to Appendices
La Gorgue	1.3.17	—	Situation normal.	
"	2.3.17	—	S/Sjt Sapp Cox G.C. reinforcement for Signal Depot. Lieut. A Fox left for 5th Corps Signals	
"	3.3.17	,		
"	4.3.17	—	SS 8124. Sapp Taylor GC. reinforcement from Signal Depot. Situation normal. Advance Party stabled. Div. Sig office at Willeman	
"	5.3.17	—	Relief by 49th Div. Signal. Company moved to St Venant Area	
St Venant	6.3.17	—	Company moved from St Venant to Pernes	
Pernes	7.3.17	"	" to Pernes " to Le Cauroy. Sig office at Willeman closed.	
Le Cauroy	8.3.17	"	Office established at Le Cauroy.	
"	9.3.17	—	Situation normal.	
"	10.3.17	—	"	
"	11.3.17	—	"	
"	12.3.17	—	Communication established between YSC and 169th Bde in line	
"	13.3.17	—	Situation normal.	
"	14.3.17	—	"	
"	15.3.17	—	7th Corps Buried System in Achicourt taken over	
"	16.3.17	—	Situation normal. Lieut. R.D. Stebbens reported for duty as offr i/c Div. Arty Gp from 5th Div. Sig Co	

Army Form C. 2118.

WAR DIARY
or
INTELLIGENCE SUMMARY.

(Erase heading not required.)

Instructions regarding War Diaries and Intelligence Summaries are contained in F. S. Regs., Part II. and the Staff Manual respectively. Title pages will be prepared in manuscript.

Place	Date	Hour	Summary of Events and Information	Remarks and references to Appendices
LE CAUROY	17.3.17	—	Rear Park left at LE CAUROY. Main body moved to SIMENCOURT.	
SIMENCOURT	18.3.17	—	Communication established with 7 CORPS.	
BEAUMETZ	19.3.17	—	Office at SIMENCOURT closed. Divnl Hqrs opened at BEAUMETZ 11am	
"	20.3.17	—	Communication established with 197th Bde. & bn hrs	
"	21.3.17	—	Situation normal.	
"	22.3.17	—	Situation normal.	
"	23.3.17	—	"	
"	24.3.17	—	"	
"	25.3.17	—	LIEUT. H.E.T. VANE transferred to "R" Corps. Sig. Co.	
"	26.2.17	—	4433 Sap SPARKS H.F. 576398 DR SMITH W.R. reinforcements for Sig Depot	
"	27.3.17	—	LIEUT H.I. MASLIN evacuated to CCS.	
"	28.3.17	—	Situation normal.	
"	29.3.17	—	"	
"	30.3.17	—	"	
"	31.3.17	—	"	

O.C. 66th Div. Sig. Coy.

66th DIVISIONAL SIGNAL COMPANY R.E.

WAR DIARY
or
INTELLIGENCE SUMMARY.

(Erase heading not required.)

Army Form C. 2118.

Vol 15

56 Divisional Signal Coy
R.E.

Place	Date	Hour	Summary of Events and Information	Remarks and references to Appendices
BEAUMETZ	1.4.17.		Establishing communications to Advd Bde H.Q. BEAURAINS.	GK
BEAUMETZ	2.4.17.		Situation normal. Major G C Kennard returned to duty from Hospital	GK
BEAUMETZ	3.4.17		Situation normal. Laying buried routes to Beaurains	GK
BEAUMETZ	4.4.17		Situation normal	GK
BEAUMETZ	5.4.17		Great shortage of cable & poles & the utmost difficulty in obtaining either from VII Corps for Artillery & Infantry	GK
BEAUMETZ	6.4.17		5 line Comic air line route established from BEAU METZ to SIMENCOURT.	GK
Beaumetz	7.4.17		Communication established from G Dugout achieved Divisional Headquarters to 167 Bde HQ and 168 Bde HQ BEAURAINS advanced BEAURAINS M3 c 45 35	GK
BEAUMETZ	8.4.17		Advanced Divisional Headquarters G Dugouts opened. ACHICOURT heavily bombarded by enemy.	GK
BEAUMETZ	9.4.17		VII Corps attack commenced at 5·30 AM	GK

Gordon Kennard
Major RE
OC Signal 56 Division

Army Form C. 2118.

WAR DIARY
or
INTELLIGENCE SUMMARY.
(Erase heading not required.)

56 Divisional Signal Co RE

Place	Date	Hour	Summary of Events and Information	Remarks and references to Appendices
G Achicourt	9/4/17		Jerusan captured its objectives. Visual established forward & lines laid. Tanks came trouble with lines for a time. Power Buzzers & Amplifiers of no value as the amplifiers in the forward rush when Battalion HQ moved got damaged. Wireless working well but not used would have relieved pressure on telegraphic lines had it been used. recently for using code the great objection. Overhauling lines	9K 9K
Achicourt	10.4.17.			
Achicourt	11.4.17		169 BDE relieved 167 Bde. at BEAURAINS. 167 BDE Moving to HOPE ST M3 D22 Communication established	9K
Achicourt	11.4.17		168 BDE HQ Established at NEUVILLE VITASSE. Lines laid & communication established VISUAL. WIRELESS. TELEGRAPH & TELEPHONE	9K
Achicourt	12.4.17		HENINEL CAPTURED	9K

Gordon Kennard
Major RE
OC Signals 56 Division

Army Form C. 2118.

WAR DIARY
or
INTELLIGENCE SUMMARY.

(Erase heading not required.)

Instructions regarding War Diaries and Intelligence Summaries are contained in F. S. Regs., Part II and the Staff Manual respectively. Title pages will be prepared in manuscript.

Place	Date	Hour	Summary of Events and Information	Remarks and references to Appendices
ACHICOURT	13/4/17		Established communication to BDE Headquarters HENINEL TELEPHONE TELEGRAPH WIRELESS & VISUAL.	9K
ACHICOURT	14/4/17	3 AM	Enemy counter attacked. Lines severely cut about but through by telegraph or telephone & visual to 169 Bde who bore the brunt of this attack. Enemy driven back.	9K 9K 9K 9K
	4pm 14/4/17		169 Bde relieved by 168 Bde at HENINEL	9K
			168 returned to NEUVILLE VITASSE	9K
ACHICOURT	15/4/17		167 Bde relieved 169 Bde at NEUVILLE VITASSE	9K
			169 Bde returning to ACHICOURT	9K
	15/4/17		2nd LIEUT H I MASLIN to ENGLAND sick	
ACHICOURT	16/4/17		Situation normal Counter attack by enemy on our Left Division	9K
ACHICOURT	17/4/17		Overhauling all lines in the forward area	9K

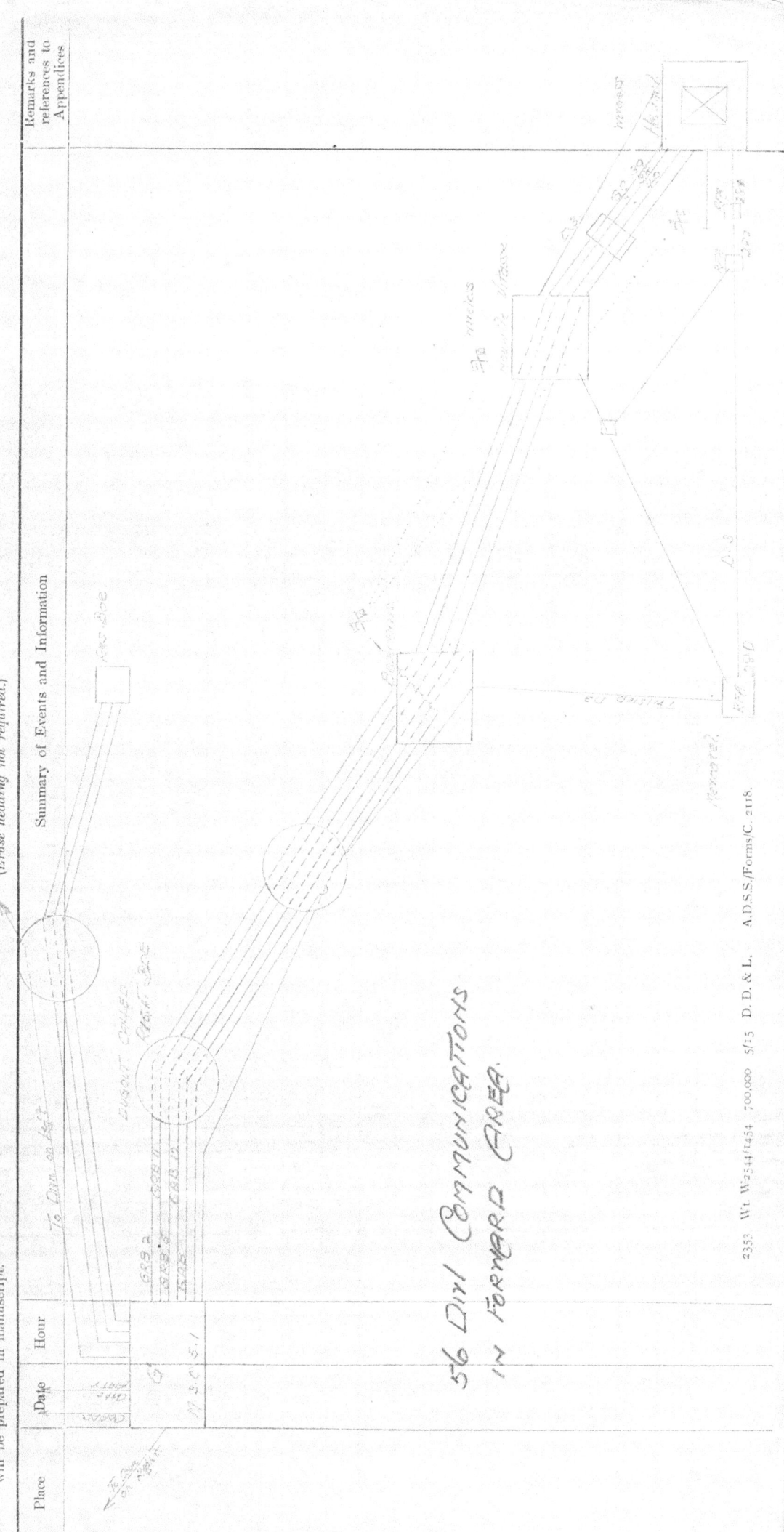

WAR DIARY
or
INTELLIGENCE SUMMARY.

(Erase heading not required.)

Army Form C. 2118.

56 Div Signal Coy RE TT

Place	Date	Hour	Summary of Events and Information	Remarks and references to Appendices
ACHICOURT	18.4.17		90th Bde of the 30th Div relieved 167 Bde in support at NEUVILLE VITASSE	Q.K.
			30th Div Sigs looked over lines before taking over	Q.K.
			Advance party left for COUIN by motor lorry to establish communications with 18th Corps & billetting areas of 167 168 & 169 BDE	Q.K. Q.K.
ALMICOURT	19.4.17		Half Company left by route march for COUIN under Capt Carpenter	Q.K.
			Remainder staying on under Capt Carpenter until 30th Div Signals were established	Q.K.
"	"		30 Div Signals arrived at 10.30 AM	Q.K.
			One Cable section remained with 56 Div Arty. from 56 Signal Coy under Lt R D SHERGOLD	Q.K.
			Company arrived COUIN 5 PM	Q.K.
COUIN	20.4.17		Party remaining under Capt CARPENTER arrived in 6 PM	Q.K.
			Bdes HQ as follows 167 PAMMIER 168 COUIN 169 SOUASTRE Div HQ COUIN Communication established	Q.K. Q.K.

Gordon Kennard Major RE
OC Signals 56 Div.

Army Form C. 2118.

WAR DIARY
or
INTELLIGENCE SUMMARY.
(Erase heading not required.)

56 DIVISIONAL SIGNAL Coy RE

Instructions regarding War Diaries and Intelligence Summaries are contained in F. S. Regs, Part II and the Staff Manual respectively. Title pages will be prepared in manuscript.

Place	Date	Hour	Summary of Events and Information	Remarks and references to Appendices
COUIN	21/4/17		Overhauling all technical Equipment.	GK
COUIN	22/4/17		As above	GK
COUIN	23/4/17		167 Bde moved to GRENAS communication established 6PM	GK
COUIN	24/4/17		Parties out collecting Telegraph Poles & reeling up Cable 168 Bde moved to GOUY 169 WANQUETIN	GK
			167 LATTRE ST QUENTIN	GK
COUIN	25/4/17		Division HQ moved to HAUTEVILLE communication established to 3 BDES	GK
HAUTEVILLE	26/4/17		Bdes moved as follows 168 BDE SIEMENCOURT General HQ established at WALRUS. Established communication with three BDES	GK GK GK GK GK GK
			Eight reinforcements reported for duty	
WALRUS	27/4/17		12 OR reported 56 DIV ART SIGNALS from 18 Corps	GK
WALRUS	28/4/17		Advance Party 56 Signals departed for ARRAS	GK
WALRUS	29/4/17		Company moved by route march an hour ached outside ARRAS	

Rear Party AD. D. & I.T. RE reconnoitring at WALRUS 29/4/17
OC Signals 56 Div, Gordon Kennard Major RET

WAR DIARY
INTELLIGENCE SUMMARY.

56 DIV SIGNALS RE(TF)

Army Form C. 2118.

Place	Date	Hour	Summary of Events and Information	Remarks and references to Appendices
ARRAS	30/4/17	10 A.M.	Took over communications (telegraph) from 15 Divisional signals. All lines in every bad condition. No telephonic communication to advanced bde 167 in line.	9K

G Kennard
Major RE
O C Signals
56 Division

Army Form C. 2118.

WAR DIARY
or
INTELLIGENCE SUMMARY.
(Erase heading not required.)

56 Divisional Signals Vol 16

Place	Date	Hour	Summary of Events and Information	Remarks and references to Appendices
ARRAS	1.5.17		Relaying all lines in forward area. LADDERING CABLE to each BDE in LINE. POLLING Telephone Routes, establishing Test points & advanced Exchange, Runner Post Motor Cyclist Post VISUAL STATIONS	Q.K.
ARRAS	2.5.17		Communications completed as per attached Diagram. 168 BDE moved from ARRAS to TILLOY.	Q.K.
ARRAS.	3.5.17		Operations by 167 Bde and 169 Bde.	Q.K.
ARRAS	4.3.17		168 Bde relieved 167 + 169 Bde. who returned to TILLOY	Q.K. Q.K.
ARRAS	5.3.17		Situation normal. Shelling considerably continuous between Gervion #9 & Boles. Lines destroyed on several occasions. Repaired & communication maintained	Q.K.
ARRAS	6.3.17		Situation normal. Shelling continued	

Gordon Kennard
Major R.E.
O.C. Signals 56 Division

Army Form C. 2118.

WAR DIARY
or
INTELLIGENCE SUMMARY.

(Erase heading not required.)

56 Divisional Signal Coy RE (77)

Place	Date	Hour	Summary of Events and Information	Remarks and references to Appendices
ARRAS	7/5/17		Situation normal	GK
ARRAS	8/5/17		Situation normal	GK
ARRAS	9/5/17		Situation normal all lines overhauled	GK
ARRAS	10/5/17		Situation normal. Corp F J Baker Rgt No 558086 awarded Military medal for gallantry in the Field by Corps Commander.	GK
ARRAS	11/5/17	8 PM	168 Bde operations objectives taken Communications extended by Bde signals concerned	GK
ARRAS	12/5/17		Situation normal	GK
ARRAS	13/5/17		All working parties engaged in burying armoured cable for Corps to Henry artillery observing stations N 24 B south of GUEMAPPE. HEAVY shelling no casualties	GK
ARRAS	14/5/17		167 Bde relieved 168 Bde. Coy engaged as about. Gordon Kennedy Major RE OC Signals 56 Division	GK

WAR DIARY
INTELLIGENCE SUMMARY

Army Form C. 2118.

56 Divisional Signal Coy R.E.(T.F.)

Place	Date	Hour	Summary of Events and Information	Remarks and references to Appendices
H⁺⁵ ARRAS	14/5/17		56 Divisional Signals Artillery sections returned to Company to take over 3rd Artillery Communications.	
			2 Sergeants (Sergt Cook + Wheeler) withdrawn from 167 & 168 Inf Bdes & sent to 280 RFA Bde & 281 RFA Bde to form new artillery Bde signal sections as per G.H.Q. OB/1026 J	9K 9K 9K
			Establishment of Divisional Signal Coy increased to 276 all ranks & 111 horses	9K
			2nd Lieut McINERNEY P reported for duty from 6th Corps.	9K
ARRAS	15/5/17		O C Signals 37 Division visited area previous to taking over communications.	9K

Gordon Kennard
Major R.E.
O C Signals 56 Division

Army Form C. 2118.

WAR DIARY
or
INTELLIGENCE SUMMARY.

56 Divisional Signal Coy R.E.

(Erase heading not required.)

Instructions regarding War Diaries and Intelligence Summaries are contained in F. S. Regs., Part II. and the Staff Manual respectively. Title pages will be prepared in manuscript.

Place	Date	Hour	Summary of Events and Information	Remarks and references to Appendices
ARRAS.	16.5/17		Advance party of 37th Div 1 Officer & 9 OR Reported. Overhauling all lines & repoling routes in forward area. One OR sap LUSH B.52.c.88.1. wounded. One Signaller Visual attached wounded	9 K
ARRAS	16.5.17		Continuation of work as above	9 K
ARRAS	17.5.17		Overhauling all lines to TILLOY	9 K
ARRAS	18.5.17		Established Visual signal station in Front line to send DD messages to the O.P. Divisional Station N.24.B. south of GUE MAPPE. Station shelled early, but by moving to a Plant & returning lines maintained	9 K
ARRAS	19.5.17		Small operation carried out by 167 Bde. 169 Bde moved from TILLOY to GUISPAINS Communication established	9 K 9 K —9 K

E Kemmard Major R.E.
O.C. Signals 56 Division

Army Form C. 2118.

WAR DIARY
or
INTELLIGENCE SUMMARY.
(Erase heading not required.)

56 Divisional Signal Coy R.E.

Instructions regarding War Diaries and Intelligence Summaries are contained in F.S. Regs., Part II. and the Staff Manual respectively. Title pages will be prepared in manuscript.

Place	Date	Hour	Summary of Events and Information	Remarks and references to Appendices
ARRAS	19.5.17		168 Bde moved to BERNAVILLE, communication established	GK
ARRAS	20.5.17		8 REINFORCEMENTS reported from Signal Depot. A large advance party 25 OR reported from 37 Div. Cable Detachment left with Artillery reported back from AGNY.	GK GK
ARRAS	21.5.17	10 AM	37 Division took over lines & communications at 10 AM.	GK
ARRAS	21.5.17	10 AM	Divisional Signal Coy moved by Route march to WARLUS. Communication established to three Bdes.	GK
WARLUS	22.5.17		167 Bde moved from ARRAS to DAINVILLE overhauling all technical equipment	GK GK
WARLUS	23.5.17		As above. Advance party from 61 Signals reported to take over lines	GK GK

Gordon Kennard Major RE
56 Divisional Signal Coy RE

Army Form C. 2118.

WAR DIARY
or
INTELLIGENCE SUMMARY.

56 Divisional Signal Coy R.E.

(Erase heading not required.)

Place	Date	Hour	Summary of Events and Information	Remarks and references to Appendices
WARLUS	24.5.17		Company moved by route march from WARLUS TO HABARCQ arriving 1 PM.	
HABARCQ	25.5.17		Communication established to three Bdes & Corps	9K
HABARCQ	26.5.17		Overhauling all cable & equipment.	9K
HABARCQ	27.5.17		Overhauling Technical stores Cable Wagons As above One reinforcement from Signal Depot reported	9K 9K 9K
HABARCQ	28.5.17		Cable wagons our carrying Inroad railway scheme One reinforcement from Signal depot Seven reinforcements to Somme. New war establishment from Signal Depot 2nd Lt W. Parkinson departed 10 days leave	9K 9K 9K 9K
HABARCQ	30.5.17		Nothing to report	9K
HABARCQ	31.5.17		One reinforcement Transferred from 18th LAK/C, Fus Reported	9K

G Kennard
Major R.E.
O.C. Divisional Signals 56 Division

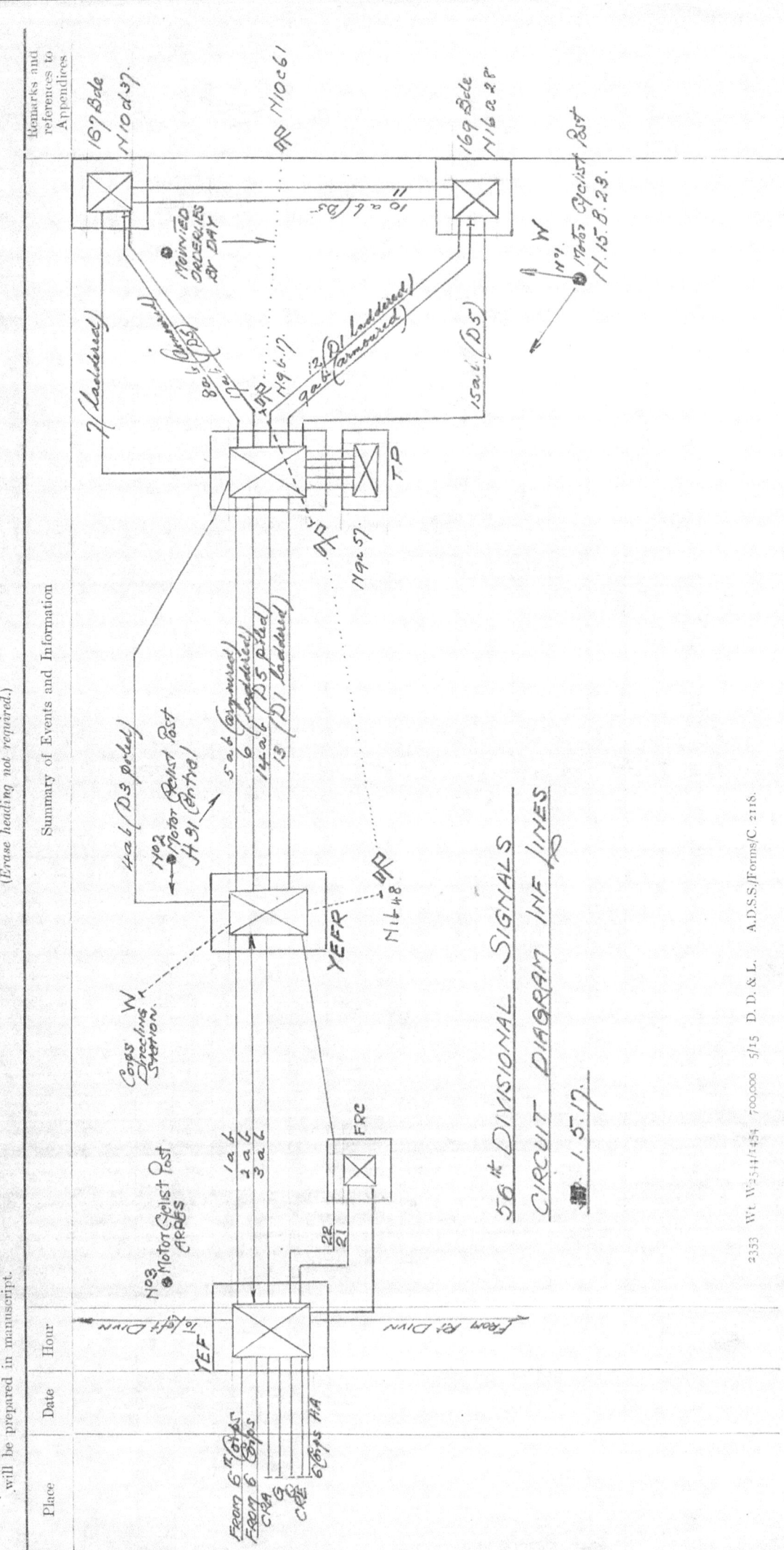

To Headquarters
56 Divn

Herewith War Diary for
June please.

Gordon Kennard
Major RE
O.C. Sigs
56th Divn

56TH (2/1ST LONDON)
SIGNAL COMPANY,
R.E. (T.)

No. K.2548.
Date 2.7.17.

Army Form C. 2118.

WAR DIARY
or
INTELLIGENCE SUMMARY.

(Erase heading not required.)

56 Divisional Signal Coy

Place	Date	Hour	Summary of Events and Information	Remarks and references to Appendices
HABARQ	1.6.17		Nothing to report	GK
HABARQ	2.6.17		Inspection of HQ - No 1 Sections by CRE	GK
HEBARCQ	3.6.17		The following NCO's & men were awarded Military Medals by the Corps Commander belonging to this Company	GK
			74211 L/C CF TARGET	GT
			5-5-8566 A/L/C FD PEASE	GT
			55-8485 SAPPER TD HARDING	GT
			55-8149 SAPPER SF LONG	GT
			55-8436 SAPPER G BRADSHAW	GT
			SSP 347 L/Cpl. LOCK. WE	GT
HABARQ	4.6.17		Inspection of Company by G.O.C. Major General CPA Hull CB at SIMENCOURT.	GT
HABARCQ	5.6.17		Company training	GK
HABARCQ	6.6.17		Company training	
			6 officers & 24 NCO's reported for special signalling course from the Infantry of the Division	GK

Gordon Kennworth
Major RE
O C Signals 56 Division

Army Form C. 2118.

WAR DIARY
or
INTELLIGENCE SUMMARY.
(Erase heading not required.)

56 Divisional Signal (Coy R E T)

Place	Date	Hour	Summary of Events and Information	Remarks and references to Appendices
HABARCQ	7.6.17		Company training	
			Signalling School commences	9+
HABARCQ	8.6.17		Advance Party sent to ARRAS to take over communications from 61 Division	9+
			Party sent by Lorry	9+
			United area	9+
			Coy Sergeant Major J Bassett 558236 departed for Signal Depot time expired	9+
			Company training	9+
HABARCQ	9.6.17			
HABARCQ	10.6.17		All reliefs (Office Linesmen - Working parties) for Advanced Divisional Exchange at TILLOY, Test Point at AIRY CORNER & Divisional HQ at ARRAS departed under Capt GC Carpenter to take over.	9+
HABARCQ	11.6.17	1 PM	Company moved by Route march to ARRAS arriving 1 PM.	9+

Gordon Kennard
Major RE
OC Signals 56 Division

WAR DIARY
or
INTELLIGENCE SUMMARY.

(Erase heading not required.)

56 DIVISIONAL SIGNAL Coy R.E.

Army Form C. 2118.

Place	Date	Hour	Summary of Events and Information	Remarks and references to Appendices
ARRAS.	12.6.17		Communications to 167 BDE TELEGRAPH HILL 168 Bde ACHICOURT + 169 Bde N10 D75 established. Polling routes Visual established 16 Battalion Signallers reported for this permanent station work	9+
ARRAS	13.6.17		Repairing + running new lines where Company engaged.	9+
ARRAS	14.6.17		Commenced work on trenches running cable + cutting out old disused Capt Shergold returned from leave - Took over Div Arty communications	9+
ARRAS	15.6.17		2 OR slightly wounded, 1 killed Corp + Corpl Motor cyclist despatch rider in A.G.	9+
ARRAS	16.6.17		Repairing + extending lines, taking up enlisted lines + replenishing try poled routes	9+
ARRAS	17.6.17			9+
ARRAS	18.6.17		Clearing divisional Area of disused cable + work continued as above	9+

Gordon Kennedy
Major R.E.
O C Signals 5-6-8

Army Form C. 2118.

WAR DIARY
or
INTELLIGENCE SUMMARY.
(Erase heading not required.)

56 Divisional Signal Coy

Place	Date	Hour	Summary of Events and Information	Remarks and references to Appendices
ARRAS	19/6/17		Communications completed. Diagram attached. 168 Bde took over from 169 in forward area. Party of Pioneer Signallers 5th Cheshires reported for duty with Signals to assist in clearing area by direct arrangement with O.C.'s	S.T.
ARRAS	20/6/17		NCOs attached from infantry for Special course returned to their units. Officers remain for a further week. Two forward Divisional O.P. lines laid + completed	S.T. S.T. S.T. S.T.
ARRAS	21/6/17		Work continued of clearing area. 30 miles D5 collected to date	S.T. S.T.
ARRAS	22/6/17		As above	S.T.

Gordon Kennard
Major R.E.
O C Signals 56 Division

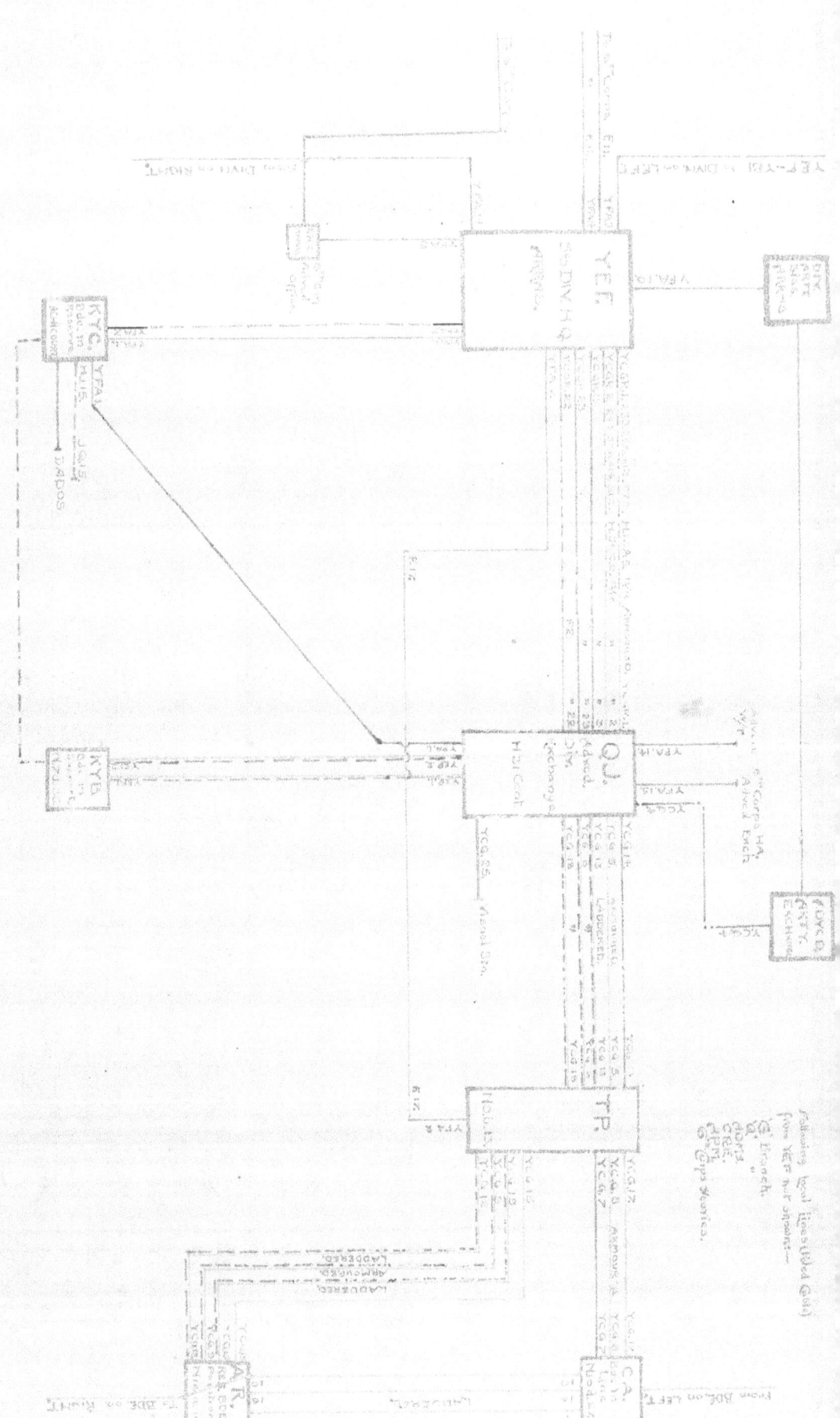

Army Form C. 2118.

WAR DIARY
or
INTELLIGENCE SUMMARY.

(Erase heading not required.)

56 Divisional Signal Coy R.E.

Instructions regarding War Diaries and Intelligence Summaries are contained in F. S. Regs., Part II. and the Staff Manual respectively. Title pages will be prepared in manuscript.

Place	Date	Hour	Summary of Events and Information	Remarks and references to Appendices
ARRAS.	23.6.17		Situation normal whole Company engaged on overhauling & cleaning also attached Churries & all Battalion signallers	9K
ARRAS	24.6.17		2nd Lieut Rayner departed in relief of 2nd Lieut McInerney in charge of Cable detachment with artillery	9K
			2nd Lieut McInerney returned to duty with Company	9K
				9K
ARRAS	25.6.17		Situation normal. 60 miles cable to hand to date commenced overhauling this run returning to 61 Div artillery & 1 B Divisional Artillery covering area	9K
ARRAS	26.6.17		OC 12 Div Sigs + OC 50 M Div Sigs arrived for conference re handing over	9K
			L. Renwood Major RE OC Signals 56 Division	

Army Form C. 2118.

WAR DIARY
or
INTELLIGENCE SUMMARY.
(Erase heading not required.)

56 Divisional Signal Co**y**

Place	Date	Hour	Summary of Events and Information	Remarks and references to Appendices
ARRAS	27/6/17		Situation normal	-G.K.
ARRAS	28/6/17		Situation normal	-G.K.
ARRAS	29/6/17		9 W/T operators transferred to Coy from 2°/17 W/T Ind section attached to VI Corps Situation normal	-G.K. -G.K.
ARRAS	30/6/17		9th Div Artillery took over from 56 Div Arty. Div Arty Signal Section moved to BEAUMETZ	G.K.

Gordon Kennard
Major RE
OC Signals 56 Division

Army Form C. 2118.

WAR DIARY
or
INTELLIGENCE SUMMARY.

(Erase heading not required.)

56 Divisional Signal Coy R.E.

Vol 1

Instructions regarding War Diaries and Intelligence Summaries are contained in F. S. Regs., Part II. and the Staff Manual respectively. Title pages will be prepared in manuscript.

Place	Date	Hour	Summary of Events and Information	Remarks and references to Appendices
ARRAS	1.7.17		Visited new Area. LE CAUROY to establish & take over communications from 12 Div.	9K
ARRAS	2.7.17		Capt G E Carpenter departed for leave. 2nd Lieut Aldridge reverted from 167 Bde to take over.	9K
ARRAS	3.7.17		Advance party in charge of 2nd Lieut Aldridge left to establish communications at LE CAUROY	9K
ARRAS	4.7.17	10.30 AM	Company left by route march for LE CAUROY at 10.30 AM arriving 6.15 PM. Divisional HQ closed at ARRAS opened at LE CAUROY. Communications established to all Brigades & Brigade stations Divisional Signals as follows	9K
LE CAUROY	5/7/17		167 IVERNEY. 168 LIGNERIEUL. 169 SUS - ST LEGER Divisional observers School connecting of 2/5 O R in Vernal	9K
LE CAUROY	6.7.17		Testing commenced	9K
LE CAUROY	7.7.17		Overhauling & reissuing equipment to Bde sections Training & as above	9K

Gordon Kennard
Major R E +
O C Signals
56 Division

Army Form C. 2118.

WAR DIARY
or
INTELLIGENCE SUMMARY.
(Erase heading not required.)

56 Divisional Signal Coy RE.

Instructions regarding War Diaries and Intelligence Summaries are contained in F. S. Regs., Part II. and the Staff Manual respectively. Title pages will be prepared in manuscript.

Place	Date	Hour	Summary of Events and Information	Remarks and references to Appendices
LE CAUROY	8/7/17		Termination of course for Battalion Signallers. All returned to their Respective units	9K
LE CAUROY	9/7/17		Company routine.	9K
LE CAUROY	10/7/17		Company sports.	9K
LE CAUROY	11/7/17		Company sports.	9K
LE CAUROY	12/7/17		Company Training. All Sappers, Pioneers & Operators commence seven day course Riding & Driving. Visual Class commences for 9th Hq & Bde Sections. Remainder of Company Training	9K 9/5 9K
LE CAUROY	13/7/17		Wireless Section formed & Apparatus distributed & overhauled	9K
LE CAUROY	14/7/17		2nd Lieut G W Aldridge departs for leave Capt G E Carpenter returns from leave	9K 9K
LE CAUROY	16/7/17		Wireless Section commences tour of Bdes 16] for instructional purposes, remaining two days with each Brigade; Battalion signallers called in to Bdes to work with them	9K

Gordon Kennard
Major RE
OC Signals 56 Division

Army Form C. 2118.

WAR DIARY
or
INTELLIGENCE SUMMARY.
(Erase heading not required.)

56 Divisional Signal Co. R.E.

Place	Date	Hour	Summary of Events and Information	Remarks and references to Appendices
LE CAUROY	16/7/17		Company training	9K
	17/7/17		Proceedings by Field General Court Martial on Driver Price R/9492575 for army abusive language to an superior officer (Sergt Murphy & 9K	9K
LE CAUROY	17/7/17		Company training	9K
LE CAUROY	18/7/17		Company training	9K
LE CAUROY	19/7/17		Company training	9K
LE CAUROY	20/7/17		Company training	9K
LE CAUROY	21/7/17		Divisional Reserves class visual signalling terminates. OR concerned return to Divisional HQ.	9K
LE CAUROY	22/7/17		Battalion Signallers Officers course terminates. officers concerned to return to Battalion. Advanced party in charge Capt Carpenter depart for Eperlecques	9K 9K 9K
LE CAUROY	23/7/17	6.20PM	Company entrained from FREVENT	9K
		10.30PM	Company detrained at ARQUES	9K
ARQUES	24/7/17	1 AM	Company moved by route march to EPERLECQUES arriving 3.30AM. Bivouacked for night	9K

L Kennard
Major R.E.
O C 56 signals 56 Division

Army Form C. 2118.

WAR DIARY
or
INTELLIGENCE SUMMARY.

(Erase heading not required.)

56 Divisional Signal Coy RE

Instructions regarding War Diaries and Intelligence Summaries are contained in F. S. Regs., Part II. and the Staff Manual respectively. Title pages will be prepared in manuscript.

Place	Date	Hour	Summary of Events and Information	Remarks and references to Appendices
EPERLECQUES	26.7.17		Extending communication to Battn	
			167. SERQUES 168 HOULLE. 169 EPERLECQUES	4K
EPERLECQUES	26.7.17		169 Bde move from EPERLECQUES to NORDAUSQUES communication established	4K
EPERLECQUES	27.7.17		Wireless & Power Buzzer course for Battalion Signallers of 168 & 167 Bde commences Battalions sending in to Division for two days. Officer Sergeant & 25 Signallers. Course to last two days	
			Battalion at a time 8th MIDDX & KENSINGTONS for instruction	4K
			2nd Lieut C F Clark evacuated to General Hospital	4K
E PERLECQUES	28.7.17		2nd Lieut P J M INERNEY took over position attached to 168 Infantry BDE	4K
EPERLECQUES	29.7.17		2nd Lieut T W ALDRIDGE to Central Wireless School for instruction + course	4K
EPERLECQUES	30.7.17		RANGERS & 4th MIDDX. Company Training	
			2nd Lieut Ward Rat Sig officer reported for 10 day course	4K
			RANGERS	

E Kennard
Major RE
OC Signals 56 Division

Army Form C. 2118.

WAR DIARY
or
INTELLIGENCE SUMMARY.

56 Divisional Signal Co RE

(Erase heading not required.)

Place	Date	Hour	Summary of Events and Information	Remarks and references to Appendices
EBERLECQUES	31.7.19		Training with Battalion regullers.	C/R

G Kennard
Major R.E.
O C Signals
5 6 Division.

Headmaster
56 Div

Herewith the
diary for August
17

G Kennard
Major
OC 1/5
S Bn

2/9/17

Army Form C. 2118.

WAR DIARY
or
INTELLIGENCE SUMMARY.
(Erase heading not required.)

August 1st 56 Div Sig Co R.E.

Place	Date	Hour	Summary of Events and Information	Remarks and references to Appendices
EPERLECQUES	1	-	Training	GK
EPERLECQUES	2		Scheme with Infantry Brigadiers of Division	GK
EPERLECQUES	3		Visited 2nd Corps Forward Area. Company Training	GK
			3rd London Signallers Scheme with Divisional Signals	GK
EPERLECQUE	4		2 OR wounded attached to RFA SUB SECTIONS	GK
			Company pushing all stores etc	GK
EPERLECQUE	5	6.30AM	Advance Party left for RENINGHELST	GK
			TRANSPORT left by route march for NOORDPEENE arriving	
			4 PM also Company. 2nd LIEUT Mc C IVOR E.A.R. reported for duty	GK
NOORDPEENE	6	30am	Company left by route march to RENINGHELST	
			arriving 12 Midday	GK
RENINGHELST	7		Situation normal	GK
RENINGHELST	8		Visited 18 TH area to take over	GK
RENINGHELST	9		2nd Lieut ALDRIDGE returned from Corps Central wireless School	GK
			Situation normal	
RENINGHELST	10		Situation normal	GK

G Kennard
Major RE
OC Signals 56 Division

Army Form C. 2118.

WAR DIARY
or
INTELLIGENCE SUMMARY.
(Erase heading not required.)

56 Divisional Signal Coy

Instructions regarding War Diaries and Intelligence Summaries are contained in F. S. Regs., Part II. and the Staff Manual respectively. Title pages will be prepared in manuscript.

Place	Date	Hour	Summary of Events and Information	Remarks and references to Appendices
RENINGHELST	11		Advance party leave by Lorry for 18th Div H27 & 68	S.K.
RENINGHELST H27 & 68 Halfway House	12	10 AM	Div HQ closed RENINGHELST & opened at H27 & 68	S.K.
H27 & 68	13		Establishing new Communications & overhauling OBL	
			Bde HQ's HALFWAY HOUSE DORMY HOUSE & H27 & 68	S.K.
			3 Bdes in line one in reserve	
H27 & 68 RENINGHELST	14		Establishing Wireless & Visual as per Diagram attached	S.K.
H27 & 68 RENINGHELST	15		Y Day Company working as above	S.K.
H27 & 68	16		Division attacked at 4.45 a.m.	S.K.
H27 & 68	17		O C 14 Divisional visited area to take over	S.K.
H27 B 68	18		Division HA moved to RENINGHELST	S.K.
RENINGHELST	19		Collecting technical equipment. Linesman left up the line at 14 Divisions disposal returned. Wireless personnel not withdrawn	S.K.
RENINGHELST	19		One OR wounded by enemies aircraft	S.K.
RENINGHELST	20		Wireless personnel returned from LINE	S.K.
			POWER BUZZER Class 24 from Bat Sigs commenced 1 weeks course	

G. Hammond
Major RE
OC Signals 56 Division

Army Form C. 2118.

WAR DIARY
or
INTELLIGENCE SUMMARY.
(Erase heading not required.)

56 Divisional Signal Coy

Vol 19

Place	Date	Hour	Summary of Events and Information	Remarks and references to Appendices
RENINGHELST	21/8/17		Overhauling all equipment & redistribution of same to BDE sections	GK
RENINGHELST	22/8/17		ADVANCE PARTY leave by MOTOR LORRY for EPERLEQUES	GK
RENINGHELST	23/8/17		Company less rear party & Sappers (DISMOUNTED) left by route march for ARNEKE & continued following day to EPERLEQUES	GK
RENINGHELST	24/8/17		Office HQ established at EPERLEQUES. 3 BDES established. Div Observers Signalling School commences	GK
EPERLEQUES	25/8/17		Situation normal Company training	GK
EPERLEQUES	26/8/17		Situation normal Company training	GK
EPERLEQUES	27/8/17		Situation normal Company training	GK
EPERLEQUES	28/8/17		ADVANCE PARTY by MOTOR LORRY to FREMICOURT Power Buzzer Class returned to Battalions	GK
EPERLEQUES	29/8/17		Situation normal	GK
EPERLEQUES	30/8/17		Company entrained for FREMICOURT	GK
FREMICOURT	31/8/17		Establishing communication to Bdes &c	GK

Gordon Kennersal
Major RE
O.C. Signals 56 Division

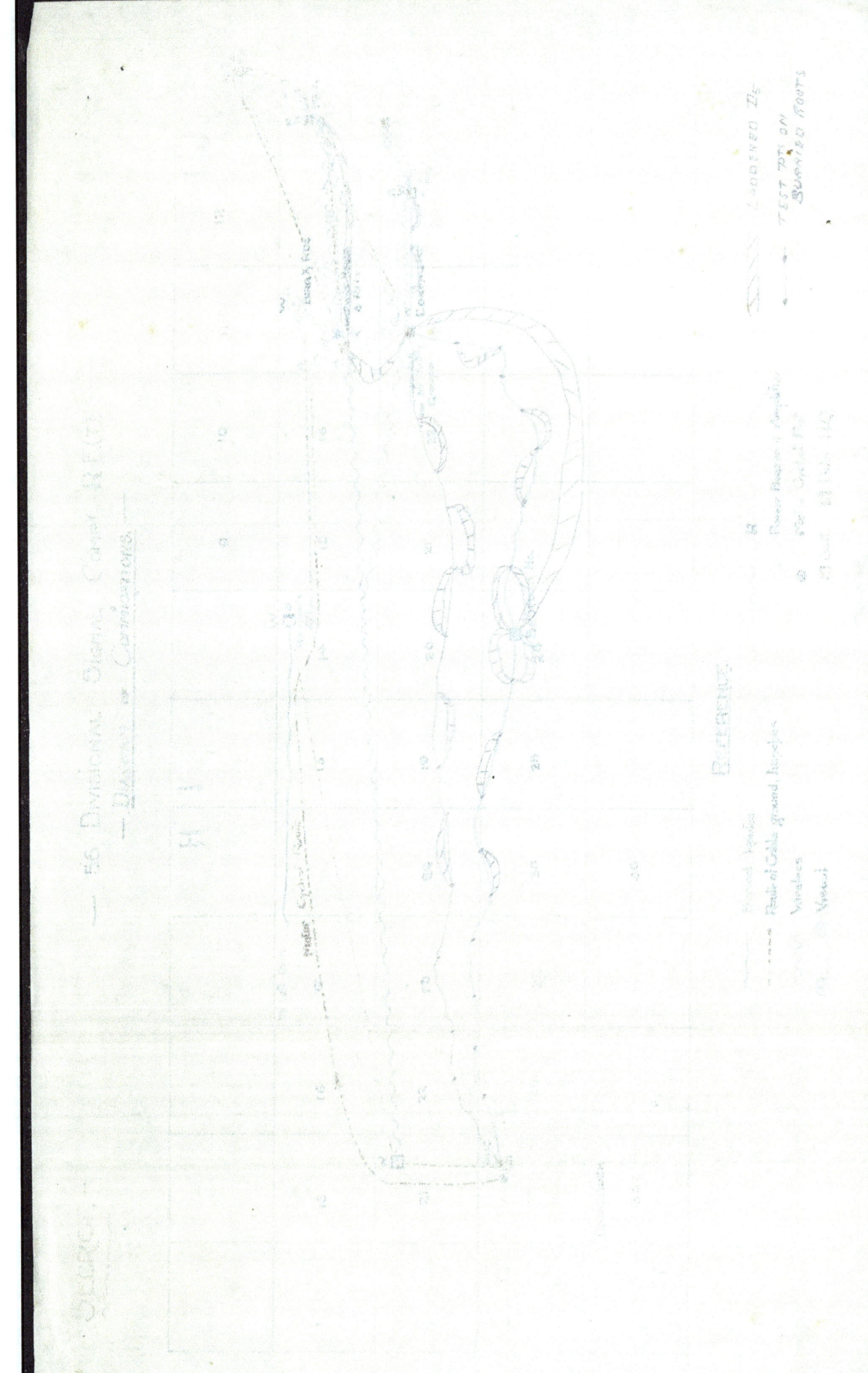

Army Form C. 2118.

WAR DIARY
or
INTELLIGENCE SUMMARY.
(Erase heading not required.)

56th Divisional Signal Coy

VOL 20

Place	Date	Hour	Summary of Events and Information	Remarks and references to Appendices
FREMICOURT	1/9/17		Communication established to 3 Bdes.	g.r.
			Connecting + installing all Local Lines	g.r.
			Building Quarters + stables	g.r.
FREMICOURT	2/9/17		As above	g.r.
FREMICOURT	3/9/17		As above Connecting up ARTILLERY LOCAL Lines + Forcing offices	g.r.
FREMICOURT	4/9/17		Overhauling all Technical Stores + Overhauling lines to Forward area which were to be taken over from 3rd Division	g.r.
FREMICOURT	5/9/17		Jigging test points for linemen in Forward area Relief of Wireless personal — Stores carried out Overhauling lines	g.r. g.r. g.r.
FREMICOURT	6/9/17		Capt G.P. Carpenter awarded Military Cross 558006 Sergt Nightingale S.T. awarded Military Medal	g.r. g.r.
FREMICOURT	7/9/17		Took over Communications + Line from 3rd Division HQ remaining at FREMICOURT	g.r. g.r.

L Renward Major RE
O C Signals 56 Division

Army Form C. 2118.

WAR DIARY
or
INTELLIGENCE SUMMARY.
(Erase heading not required.)

56 Divisional Signal Coy.

Instructions regarding War Diaries and Intelligence Summaries are contained in F. S. Regs., Part II. and the Staff Manual respectively. Title pages will be prepared in manuscript.

Place	Date	Hour	Summary of Events and Information	Remarks and references to Appendices
FREMICOURT	8/9/17		Sergt Gomell A.E. 55-8245 awarded Military Medal took over prepared Test pts from 300 pr 170. VH + IX. All Company working on staying up routes & overhauling all lines forward area	GK
FREMICOURT	9/9/17		As above situation normal	GK
FREMICOURT	10/9/17		2nd/T F.C. Clarke returned from Hospital. Work as above situation normal	GK GK
FREMICOURT	11/9/17		Major Gordon Cecil Kennard departed for leave Capt G.E. Carpenter took over. Work proceeding as above situation normal	GK
FREMICOURT	12/9/17		Work as above situation normal	GK
FREMICOURT	13/9/17		2nd/T F.C. Clarke took over Bde Section 168 Bde. 2nd/LT 1st INERNEY P returning to Division	GK
FREMICOURT	14/9/17		Work as usual Situation normal	GK
FREMICOURT	15/9/17		Rg 90 530546 Pease F.O. A/L me/Corp arrived II CM. Work as usual situation normal	GK

Gordon Kennard
Major RE
OC Signals 56 Division

Army Form C. 2118.

WAR DIARY
or
INTELLIGENCE SUMMARY.
(Erase heading not required.)

56 Divisional Signal Coy.

Place	Date	Hour	Summary of Events and Information	Remarks and references to Appendices
FREMICOURT	16/9/17		No 558802 Corporal H.F. Page. 558068 Corp A.L. MUNDEN 198149 A/CP R B DICKIE 558967 L/Cpl C A Bailey 558/24 Sapper G C TAYLOR awarded military medal	gt gt gt
FREMICOURT	16/9/17		Work as usual. Situation normal	gt
"			Line work. Situation normal	gt
FREMICOURT	17/9/17		2 Reinforcements from Signal Depot. Overhauling & repairing all existing air line routes - relaying of lines in forward area - taking of future Engineering Communications & laying of laterals between Bde & Battalions as above. Situation normal	gt
FREMICOURT	18/9/17		As above situation normal	gt
"			Ground lines & all P.B. Case line dug in & buried. That up at all wireless stations amplifier - Power Buzzer stations	gt
FREMICOURT	19/9/17			gt

Gordon Kennard
Major R.E.
O.C. Signals 56 Division

Army Form C. 2118.

WAR DIARY
or
INTELLIGENCE SUMMARY.
(Erase heading not required.)

56 Divisional Signal Coy RE

Place	Date	Hour	Summary of Events and Information	Remarks and references to Appendices
FREMICOURT	21/9/17		5-58512 Sapper E Blackwell 5-58640 Pioneer Staines & 5-58984 Sapper H Roe 5-58L11 Lance Corp H7 Hudson awarded Military Medal for recent operations. Getting out new lines SOS + company. Situation normal	GR GR GR
FREMICOURT	22/9/17		2nd Lieut RAYNER J VR posted to 2.091 Maintenance Party 2nd ARMY. 2nd Lieut /Me INTERNEY R to GHQ Wireless Course 55-8348 Sergt WW WELLER to GHQ Wireless course commencing 28th. Continuation of SOS Coy + Battery Lines relaying of same	GR GR GR GR
FREMICOURT	23/9/17		Major G C Kenward returned from Leave. Work on Lines to Battalions continued. Situation normal	GR GR GR

Gordon Kenward
Major RE
OC Signals
56 Divisional

Army Form C. 2118.

WAR DIARY
or
INTELLIGENCE SUMMARY
(Erase heading not required.)

56 Divisional Signal Coy

Place	Date	Hour	Summary of Events and Information	Remarks and references to Appendices
FREMICOURT	24/9/17		Working on Lines Forward Area Situation normal	SK
FREMICOURT	25/9/17		As above situation normal	SK
FREMICOURT	26/9/17		Capt RA Shergold granted 10 days leave departed	SK
	26/9/17		Situation normal	SK
			Capt G.E. Carpenter M.C. departed for command 40th Div Signal Coy	SK
			Capt RA Shergold (second in command of 56 Signals)	SK
FREMICOURT	27/9/17		Situation normal	SK
			Divisional Signalling School Commenced 2 men from each Battalion + 2 men from each Battery	SK
			report Total 40	SK
			Situation normal	SK
FREMICOURT	28/9/17		Overhauling of L.B.M.U routes + resurveying of same	SK
			Digging in communication trench to Left + Rt Coy's left	SK
			Side Scoter for buried Cable route Commenced	SK
			London Kennard	
			O.C Signals 56 Div.RE	

Army Form C. 2118.

WAR DIARY
or
INTELLIGENCE SUMMARY
(Erase heading not required.)

56 Divisional Signal Coy RE

Place	Date	Hour	Summary of Events and Information	Remarks and references to Appendices
FRENICOURT	3/9/17		New Routes to Centre Bdes & Groupes commenced Situation normal	G.R.
			Diagram of Communications for Divisional Lines to Bdes & Groupes attached.	G.R.

Gordon Kennard
Major RE
O C Signals
56 Division

SECRET

56th Divisional Signal Office Circuit Diagram

○ INF BDES
○ ART GROUPS

50TH (2/1ST LONDON)
SIGNAL COMPANY,
R.E. (T.)
No..........
Date..........

- LA (I.N.C.ess.) — left Bde, Morchies
- MO-LA route
- R.Bde.
- BZ (I20C.2.?) — R.Bde.
- Pitre Bde.
- MO
- LB
- VU (I36a.7.8. AD Exchange) — Albuquerque, Velu, VU–SL route, HP–VU route
- FT–MO route, Beugny
- DX (I33a.8.2.) — DX–LB route
- SIGS ADYD DIV HQRS (I34a.3.4.)
- DA (I34a.4.4.)
- HP — Sunk'n C., HP–RX, O.4.a.6.9.
- HT 0.3.d.4.9
- FT (I35.8.4.) — Divisional Headquarters, Fremicourt
- FT–HP route
- BN–DX, Barastre
- BN (H.35.C.ess.)
- BC (N.R.C.ert.) — BC–HP route, S.?

Army Form C. 2118.

WAR DIARY
or
INTELLIGENCE SUMMARY
(Erase heading not required.)

56 Divisional Signal Coy R.E.

Place	Date	Hour	Summary of Events and Information	Remarks and references to Appendices
FREMICOURT	1/10/17		Situation normal. Work on lines proceeding	G.S. / G.S.
FREMICOURT	2/10/17		Lt R.G. Larking M.C. from P Corps Signal Coy reported for duty i/c Artillery signals 56 Div. Authority G/H 9/A 55/8(0')	G.S.
FREMICOURT	3/10/17		Situation normal.	R.C.
FREMICOURT	4/10/17		Erection of new Perm - permanent G.S. route FT-FTA	R.C.
FREMICOURT	5/10/17		Continued as above.	R.C.
FREMICOURT	6/10/17		Do " " " Stabs Cable Route from MO test point to 167 Brigade. Capt. R.D. SHERGOLD from leave.	R.C.
FREMICOURT	7/10/17		MO-LA route strained up and repaired (damaged by shell fire).	R.C.
FREMICOURT	8/10/17		Poled Cable to 167 Brigade Reserve Battn relaid	R.C.

R.T. Capt.
for Major R.E.
o/c Signals
56 Div

WAR DIARY
INTELLIGENCE SUMMARY

(Erase heading not required.) 56th Divisional Signal Co. R.E.

Army Form C. 2118.

Place	Date	Hour	Summary of Events and Information	Remarks and references to Appendices
FREMICOURT	9/10/17	—	Work on new line to 193 M.G. Co. Winter quarters. New routes started and lines moved between 289th Bde R.F.A. and crossings in I.5.6. (57C N.W. 20/000) line 289th Bde to B/281 and exchange at C.22.d.6.0 dismantled. Returned MORCHIES	R.C. R.C.
FREMICOURT	10/10/17		As above. Situation Normal	R.C.
FREMICOURT	11/10/17		Do do do	R.C.
FREMICOURT	12/10/17		Lt. F.C. CLARK granted 10 days leave to U.K. Work on forward lines	R.C.
FREMICOURT	13/10/17		Work on new lines in consequence of changes in disposition of guns. Labelling and staking lines from 280 F Bde R.F.A.	R.C.
FREMICOURT	14/10/17		Situation Normal	R.C.
FREMICOURT	15/10/17		Do do	R.C.
FREMICOURT	16/10/17		Do do Lt. R.G. LARKIN G granted 10 days leave to U.K.	R.C. R.C.

R.C. / Capt.
L. Hayes R.E.
for O.C. Signals
56 Divn.

Army Form C. 2118.

WAR DIARY
or
INTELLIGENCE SUMMARY.

(Erase heading not required.) 56th Divisional Signal Co RE.

Instructions regarding War Diaries and Intelligence Summaries are contained in F. S. Regs., Part II. and the Staff Manual respectively. Title pages will be prepared in manuscript.

Place	Date	Hour	Summary of Events and Information	Remarks and references to Appendices
FREMICOURT	17/10/17		W on R in forward lines. 558006. Sgt. S.T. HIGHTINGALE, 558225 Sgt. A.E. GOSNELL proceeded to England for Commission in Signal Service.	P.C.
FREMICOURT	18/10/17		Situation Normal. Lt. R.G. KIRKING. M.C. appointed Acting Captain whilst in Command of Divl Artillery Signals.	P.C.
FREMICOURT	19/10/17		Situation Normal. 12th Signal School for Battalion and Battery Signallers concluded.	P.C.
FREMICOURT	20/10/17		W on R as usual. Situation Normal.	P.C.
FREMICOURT	21/10/17		Do do	P.C.
FREMICOURT	22/10/17		13th Signal School for Battn and Battery Signallers Commenced. New line of Armoured Cable being laid to Neath forward Battn, 169 Bde.	P.C.
FREMICOURT	23/10/17		Lt. W. PARKINSON granted 10 days leave to U.K. Overhauling of all local lines, routes wires stayed up.	P.C.

R.———— Capt
Signaller RE
O/C 56 Divn

A 5834 Wt.W4973/M687 750,000 8/16 D. D. & L. Ltd. Forms/C.2118/13.

Army Form C. 2118.

WAR DIARY
or
INTELLIGENCE SUMMARY.

(Erase heading not required.)

50th Divisional Signal Co. 887

Place	Date	Hour	Summary of Events and Information	Remarks and references to Appendices
FREMICOURT	24/10/17		Work as on 23rd inst. Signallers from A & F Staffords reported for Course.	RC
FREMICOURT	25/10/17		Lt. F.C. CLARK from leave. Work as usual. Situation Normal.	RC
FREMICOURT	26/10/17		Building of Test Point at HP and Test Point at VU Exchange.	RC
FRESNOCOURT	27/10/17		Work as above.	RC
FREMICOURT	28/10/17		Work as above. Reference to R.G. Co. Communications.	RC
FREMICOURT	29/10/17		Work on forward and local lines. Situation normal.	RC
FREMICOURT	30/10/17		Signal School for R.G. Co. Signallers Commenced (16 m).	RC
FREMICOURT	31/10/17		Situation Normal.	RC

R.P. Toon
Major RE.
OC Signals
50 Div.

C.S.O.
56 Div'n

Herewith War Diary
for November.

[stamp: 56th (1st LONDON)
SIGNAL COMPANY,
R.E. (T.)
No. K.342
1.12.17]

Major C.
O.C.
56 Div'n

Army Form C. 2118.

WAR DIARY
or
INTELLIGENCE SUMMARY.
(Erase heading not required.)

Instructions regarding War Diaries and Intelligence Summaries are contained in F.S. Regs., Part II. and the Staff Manual respectively. Title pages will be prepared in manuscript.

56 D Signals

Place	Date	Hour	Summary of Events and Information	Remarks and references to Appendices
FREMICOURT	1.11.17		Signal Conference at IV Corps. Capt Larking I/c Div ARP Sigs returned from leave	gk
FREMICOURT	2.11.17		Establishing new system of Communications as per Diagram attached.	gk
"	3.11.17		2nd Lt Inglis departed for 14 days leave Lieut W Parkinson returned from above Construction of new Routes commenced	gk
"	4.11.17		As above	gk
"	5.11.17		Work on new routes whole Company engaged	gk
"	6.11.17		As above	gk
"	7.11.17		As above	gk
"	8.11.17		Wireless School at Turmond Signals commenced	gk
"	9.11.17		Work on Forward Communications Restaying + staking lines	gk

Gordon Kennard
Major RE
OC Signals 56 Div.

Army Form C. 2118.

WAR DIARY
or
INTELLIGENCE SUMMARY.
(Erase heading not required.)

56 Divisional Signal Coy

56TH (2/1ST LONDON) SIGNAL COMPANY.
R.E. (L)

Place	Date	Hour	Summary of Events and Information	Remarks and references to Appendices
FREMICOURT	10.11.17		Wireless school returned to units	GK
			2nd Wireless school for Officers commences	GK
FREMICOURT	11.11.17		Conference at Div. H.Q.	GK
			Work on forward communications commences	GK
			One section reeling up all spare lines available	GK
"	12.11.17		2ND Lieut MacINERNEY returned from 10 days leave	GK
			Forward Exchange established at LOUVERVAL	GK
			Communication line work continued	GK
"	13.11.17		As above	GK
"	14.11.17		As above	GK
"	15.11.17		As above	GK
"	16.11.17		As above	GK
"	17.11.17		As above	GK
"	18.11.17		All new system tested through & work completed	GK

Gordon Kennard
Major RE
O Signals 56 Div

Army Form C. 2118.

WAR DIARY
or
INTELLIGENCE SUMMARY.
(Erase heading not required.)

56TH (2/1ST LONDON)
SIGNAL COMPANY.
R.E. (T.)

Instructions regarding War Diaries and Intelligence Summaries are contained in F. S. Regs., Part II. and the Staff Manual respectively. Title pages will be prepared in manuscript.

Place	Date	Hour	Summary of Events and Information	Remarks and references to Appendices

56TH DIVISIONAL SIGNALS
ROUTE DIAGRAM OF COMMUNICATIONS
— — — Call
———— On Line

Locations shown: FREMICOURT, MORCHIES, C.29.a.4.3, LAGNICOURT, C.24.c.8.4, I.11.c.4.7, I.11.b.4.3, T.1.a.8.8, LOUVERVAL, BEAUMETZ, J.17.a.4.8, J.20.c.6.1, J.28.a.2.5, J.30.a.8.6, J.36.a.8.2

A.5834. Wt. W.4973/M687. 750,000 8/15 D. D. & L. Ltd. Forms/C 2118/13.

WAR DIARY
INTELLIGENCE SUMMARY

Army Form C.

56TH (2/1ST LONDON) SIGNAL COMPANY.

56 Divisional Signal Coy

Place	Date	Hour	Summary of Events and Information	Remarks and references to Appendices
FREMICOURT	19.11.17		A C Cable section arrived in Charge of 2nd Lieuter	GK
"	20.11.17		IV Corp Operations commenced 168 Bde moved from HANEH LAGNICOURT TO BEUGNY communication established	GK
"	20.11.17		169 Bde moved to ADVANCED BDE H.Q	GK
"	21.11.17		Operations continued 40th Div. moved through area. Certain lines for their communications given over	GK
"	22.11.17		168 Bde established H Q MORCHIES. communication established	GK
"	23.11.17		Operations continued 2nd Lt Ingles returned from leave	GK GK
"	24.11.17		Operations continued	GK
"	25.11.17		Operations continued	GK
"	25.11.17		A C Cable section recalled to VI Corps.	GK

Gordon Kennard
Major R.E.
OC Signals 56 Div.

WAR DIARY or INTELLIGENCE SUMMARY

Army Form C. 2118.

56th (21st LONDON) SIGNAL COMPANY R.E. (T.)

56 Divisional Signal Co. of R.E.

Place	Date	Hour	Summary of Events and Information	Remarks and references to Appendices
FREMICOURT	26.11.17		Operations continued	G.T.
"	27.11.17		NCO & 8 OR returned from AC cable section.	G.T.
"	28.11.17		Operations continued.	G.T.
"	29.11.17		Operations continued	G.T.
"	30.11.17		Counter attack by enemy. Communication re-established.	G.T.
			Counter attack failed.	G.T.
			Wireless Station captured.	G.T.
			Recaptured & re-erected.	G.T.
			Amplifier destroyed by Wireless Personnel.	G.T.
			All secret documents burnt	G.T.
			Communication re-established	G.T.
			2nd Lieut MacInerney & 3 OR's gassed 2 OR's wounded	G.T.

Gordon Kennard
Major R.E.
O.C. Signals
56 Div.

To Headquarters
56 Div.

Herewith War Diary
for December.

[stamp: 55th (2/1st LONDON) SIGNAL COMPANY, R.E. (T.) No. I. 3255 Date 1.1.18]

R———
Capt RE
for OC Sigs
56 Div.

Army Form C. 2118.

56 D Signals

WAR DIARY
or
INTELLIGENCE SUMMARY.

(Erase heading not required.)

Instructions regarding War Diaries and Intelligence Summaries are contained in F. S. Regs., Part II. and the Staff Manual respectively. Title pages will be prepared in manuscript.

Place	Date	Hour	Summary of Events and Information	Remarks and references to Appendices
FREMICOURT	1/8/99		OC Signals 57 Divn tested over and went over lines.	RO
"	2/8/99		Advance party of 7th Div was proceeded to FOSSEUX	RO
FOSSEUX	3/8/99		Division opened at FOSSEUX 10 noon	RO
"	4/8/99		Advance party of Capt Sheppard proceeded to Victory Camp BOIRYNCOURT	RO
BOIRYNCOURT	5/8/99		Division opened at VICTORY Camp BOIRYNCOURT at 12 noon	RO
"	6/8/99		Do ditto (Situation normal)	RO
"	7/8/99		do	RO
"	8/8/99		Forward moves to BOIRYNCOURT Camp cancelled. Conference at B" Corps	RO
"	9/8/99		Situation normal	RO
"	10/8/99		do	RO
"	11/8/99		do	RO
"	12/8/99		ADSig. XIII Corps arrived	RO
"	13/8/99		Situation normal	RO
"	14/8/99		Lt Aldridge proceeded on leave	RO

R Chang
Capt
for OC Signals
56 Divn

WAR DIARY or INTELLIGENCE SUMMARY

Army Form C. 2118.

Place	Date	Hour	Summary of Events and Information	Remarks and references to Appendices
ECKINCOURT	1.2.17		Situation normal. All the wounds of Battn. proceeded to 1st Army to 3 weeks Musketry Course	
	2.2.17		do	
	3.2.17		do	
	4.2.17		do	
	5.2.17		do	
	6.2.17		do	
	7.2.17		169 Brigade in has Railway EMBKT. 167 Brigade worker to WAKEFIELD CAMP PROVINCOURT	
	8.2.17		Situation normal	
	9.2.17		do	
	10.2.17		do	
	11.2.17		do	
	12.2.17		OC proceeded on leave to NICE	
	13.2.17		167 Brigade relieved 168 Brigade	
	14.2.17		167 Brigade proceeded to Blue Line at PROVART. ST AMAND	
	15.2.17		Situation normal	
	16.2.17		do 2nd Lt Parkinson proceeded on 6 last Blue Course	
	17.2.17		do Lt Aldridge returned from leave	

B.O. / Capt RE
for O.C. Sqnebs
56 Bn.

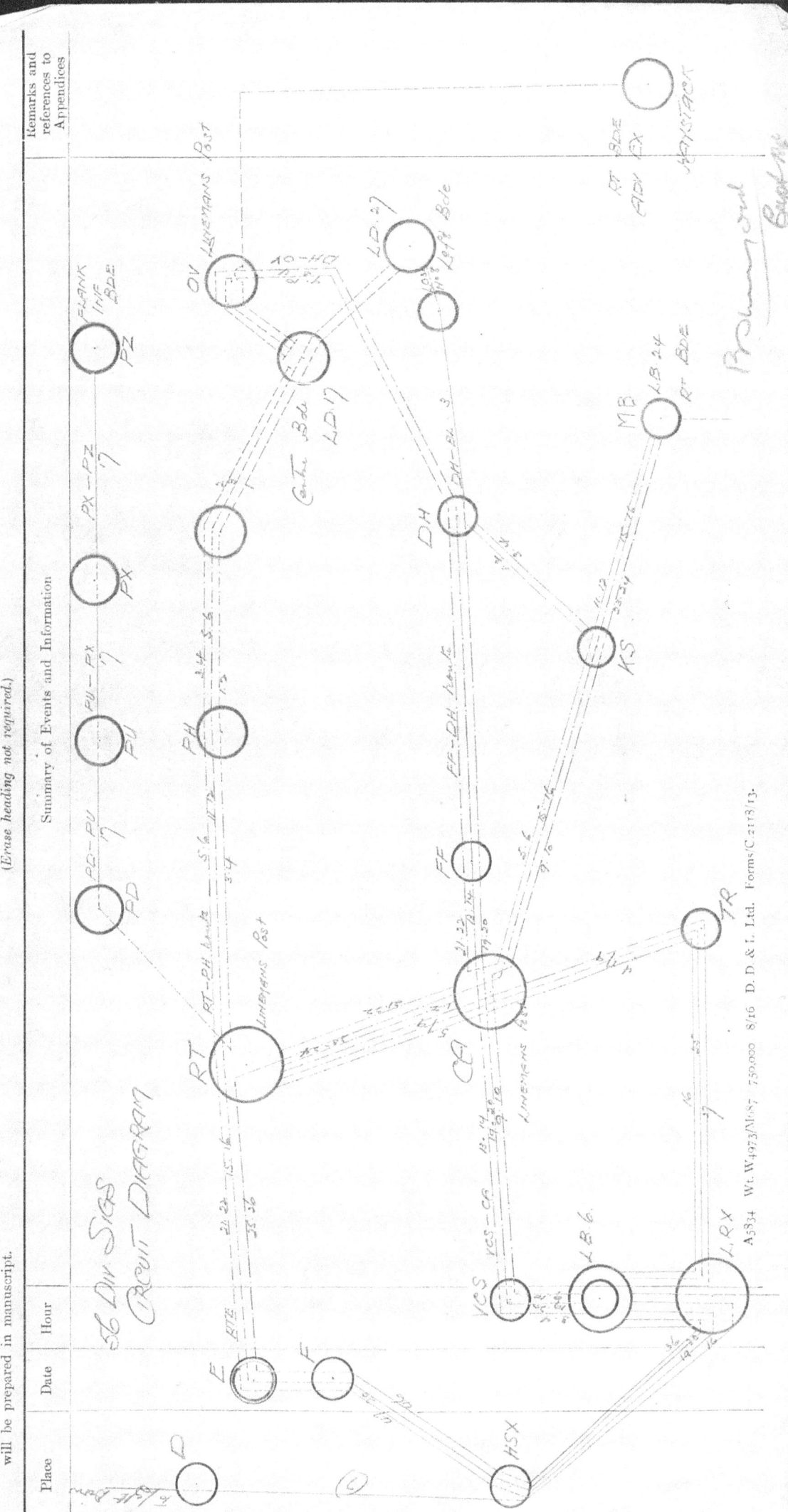

WAR DIARY or INTELLIGENCE SUMMARY

Army Form C. 2118.

56 D Signals Vol 24

Place	Date	Hour	Summary of Events and Information	Remarks and references to Appendices
VICTORY CAMP	1.1.1918		Situation normal.	RC
ROCLINCOURT				
"	2.1.1918		Lt Parkinson goes for course (Wireless Patrol) with No 5 Squadron RFC	RC
"	3.1.1918		OC 63rd Division (a) visits to arrange relief	RC
"	4.1.1918		Situation normal.	RC
"	5.1.1918		Lt Parkinson returns from course.	RC
"	6.1.1918		Capt Jarking & Lt Inglis go to 1st Army Wireless School	RC
			a/c Lt Welson & Lt Beattie return from " "	RC
"	7.1.1918		a/c Lt J.A. Walker reports for duty	RC
"	8.1.1918		Lieut Park and Wireless Section relieved by 63rd Divn.	RC
"	9.1.1918		Company relieved and move to VILLERS CHATEL. Communication established to Brigades & RAO	RC
VILLERS CHATEL	6.1.1918		Occupying alone to.	RC
			School started at Div HQ and SAVY under Lt Page, 8th Middlesex Regt	

[signature] Capt
for OC Sigs 56 Div.

Army Form C. 2118.

WAR DIARY
or
INTELLIGENCE SUMMARY.
(Erase heading not required.)

Instructions regarding War Diaries and Intelligence Summaries are contained in F. S. Regs., Part II. and the Staff Manual respectively. Title pages will be prepared in manuscript.

56 Divisional Signal Coy

Place	Date	Hour	Summary of Events and Information	Remarks and references to Appendices
VILLERS CHATEL	21/1/18		Pigeon Course for Artillery & Infantry commences 3I OR	G.L
"	22/1/18		Company Training. Lt R J Beattie granted 14 days Leave	G.L
"	23/1/18		Communication scheme.	G.L
"	24/1/18		Company Training	G.L
"	25/1/18		Company Training	G.L
"	26/1/18		All main routes to Corps & Boles down through atmospheric disturbances. All cable wagon detachments turned out 11.45 PM. & Cable run to all routes. Communication re-established 6 AM, 27th	G.L
"	27/1/18		Rebuilding main routes. Capt Larking & 2 Lt Inglis returned from Wireless Course	G.L
"	28/1/18		Rebuilding main routes continued	G.L
"	29/1/18		As above. Capt Shergold departed on 14 days leave	G.L
"	30/1/18		Rebuilding main routes	G.L
"	31/1/18			G.L

Gordon Kennedy
Major R.E.
O.C. Signals 56 Division

To
Headquarters
56th Divn

Herewith War Diary for the month of February 1918

2 March 1918

D Pinbury Capt RE
for Major RE
OC Signals
56 Divn

Army Form C. 2118.

WAR DIARY
or
INTELLIGENCE SUMMARY.
(Erase heading not required.)

5-6 Divisional Signal Coy RE

Vol 25

Place	Date	Hour	Summary of Events and Information	Remarks and references to Appendices
VILLERS CHATEL	FEB. 1.		Company Training. Visual Scheme for SubSection's Artillery.	G.K.
VILLERS CHATEL	2		Company Training	G.K.
"	3		Divisional Visual Scheme with Inf School (Signal)	G.K.
			Lt W Parkinson departed for 14 days leave	G.K.
"	4		Company Training	G.K.
"	5		14th Divisional Signal School terminated all ranks return to units	G.K.
"	6		15th Divisional Signal School commences	G.K.
			Lt R J Beattie returned from leave	
"	7		Visited 56 62 Div to arrange taking over details	G.K.
			167 Bde to the Line Reserve Area	
"	8		Company Training	G.K.
"	9		168 Bde to Reserve Area	G.K.
"	10		Company packing Advanced Signals established G3373	G.K.
"	11		Divisional HQ closed VILLERS CHATEL opened G3373	G.K.

Gordon Kennard
Major RE OC Sigs 56 Div

Army Form C. 2118.

WAR DIARY
or
INTELLIGENCE SUMMARY.
(Erase heading not required.)

56 Divisional Signal Coy RE

Place	Date	Hour	Summary of Events and Information	Remarks and references to Appendices
VILLERS CHATEL	11/2/18		Overhauling all equipment + Coy training	St
"	12/2/18		Overhauling all equipment + Coy training	St
"	13/2/18		Scheme of communication by cable waggons	St
"	14/2/18		Visual Scheme for H9 1A + 1B sections	St
"	14/2/18		Major S Kennard returned from leave. 2nd Lt W Leavey reported for duty from England	St
"	15/2/18		Company training	
"	16/2/18		Communication Scheme for Divisnl Battalion Sgs	St
"	16/2/18		School of RA Instruction personnel commences	St
"	17/2/18		Company training	St
"	18/2/18		Company training	St
"	19/2/18		Company training Visual scheme for Bat School	St
"	20/2/18		Company training	St

Gordon Kennard
Major RE
OC Signals 56 Divn

Army Form C. 2118.

WAR DIARY
INTELLIGENCE SUMMARY.
(Erase heading not required.)

56 Divisional Signal Co RE

Place	Date	Hour	Summary of Events and Information	Remarks and references to Appendices
VICTORY CAMP ROCLINCOURT 93.B.7.3.	12		Installing communications Centre Bde & getting through new Routes	GK
"	13		Capt R D Shergold returned from Leave. Company working on Communications. Visual Established to Bdes & Battalions	GK GK GK
	14		Wireless Communications arranged from Div to Posts in front line	GK
	15		Getting through Buried Routes	GK
	16		as above. 2nd Lt LEANEY F W to Wireless Course ABBEVILLE	GK GK
	17		Working on Forward Buries. Air Line Routes restrung. Lt W PARKINSON RETURNED from Leave	GK GK
	18		Lt F E CLARK departed for Leave	GK

Gordon Kennard
Major RE
OC Sigs 56 Div

WAR DIARY

INTELLIGENCE SUMMARY

5-6 Divisional Signal Coy RE

Army Form C. 2118.

Place	Date	Hour	Summary of Events and Information	Remarks and references to Appendices
VICTORY CAMP ROELINCOURT 93B73	19.		New buried routes commenced. Centre & Right Bde	EK
"	20		Buries continued 7 ft.	EK
	21		Capt D Polivay from 1st Corps Signals reported for duty	EK
			Capt R E Larkins departed for duty 1st Army Signals.	EK
	22		Capt RD Shergold took over duty in charge Artillery Signals	EK
			Capt D Polivay assumed duty as 2nd in Command	EK
			All Company less sappers engaged on visual outposts	EK
			Divisional Station, 2 & 3 Bde stations	EK
			All sappers buried Cable routes	EK
			9 Cheshire Signallers reported to maintain communication	EK
			by visual to Bdes	EK
			5 Bat Signallers from 131b Corps reinforcement camp for training	EK
	23		Work on Buried Routes, Drivers revetting Huts	EK
			Buried Routes to Right Group commenced	EK
	24		As above, buries for amplifier earths commenced	EK
			Right Bat Right Bde	
			L Kennard Major RE	
			O C Sigs 5 & 6 Div	

Army Form C. 2118.

WAR DIARY
or
INTELLIGENCE SUMMARY.
(Erase heading not required.)

569 Divisional Signal Coy RE

Place	Date	Hour	Summary of Events and Information	Remarks and references to Appendices
VICTORY CAMP ROCLINCOURT Q31393	25		Buried cable routes. New lines laid to Centre Bde & spare to Left Bde. All drivers Revetting Huts. 2nd Lieut Q & T THOMPSON reported for duty from 1st Group Army (under instruction)	G.K.
"	26		Work on Buried Test Points commenced. Buried routes to Centre & Right Bdes continued	G.K.
"	27		Spare lines to Left Bde completed. Buries continued	G.K. G.K.
"	28		15 Divisional Signal School terminated. 70 OR & 2 Officers returned to units. VISUAL. Power Buzzer & Amplifier Diagram of Lines. & IRLS. attached Wireless Runner	G.K. G.K. G.K.

Gordon Kennard
Major RE
O C Signals 56 Division

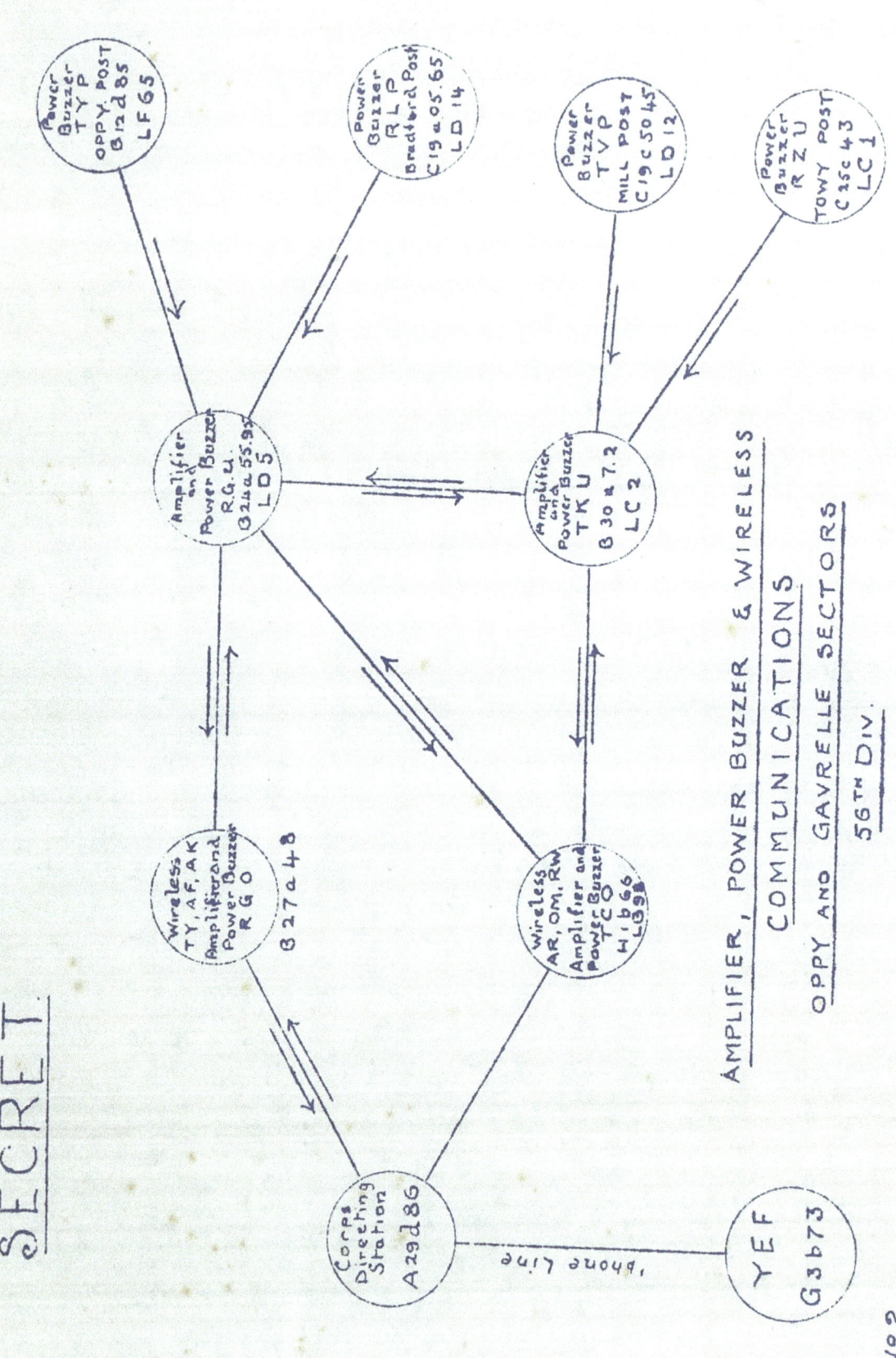

SECRET

NOTE. VISUAL re Bdes would only be brought into use on Active Operations. Forward of Bdes VISUAL tested daily.

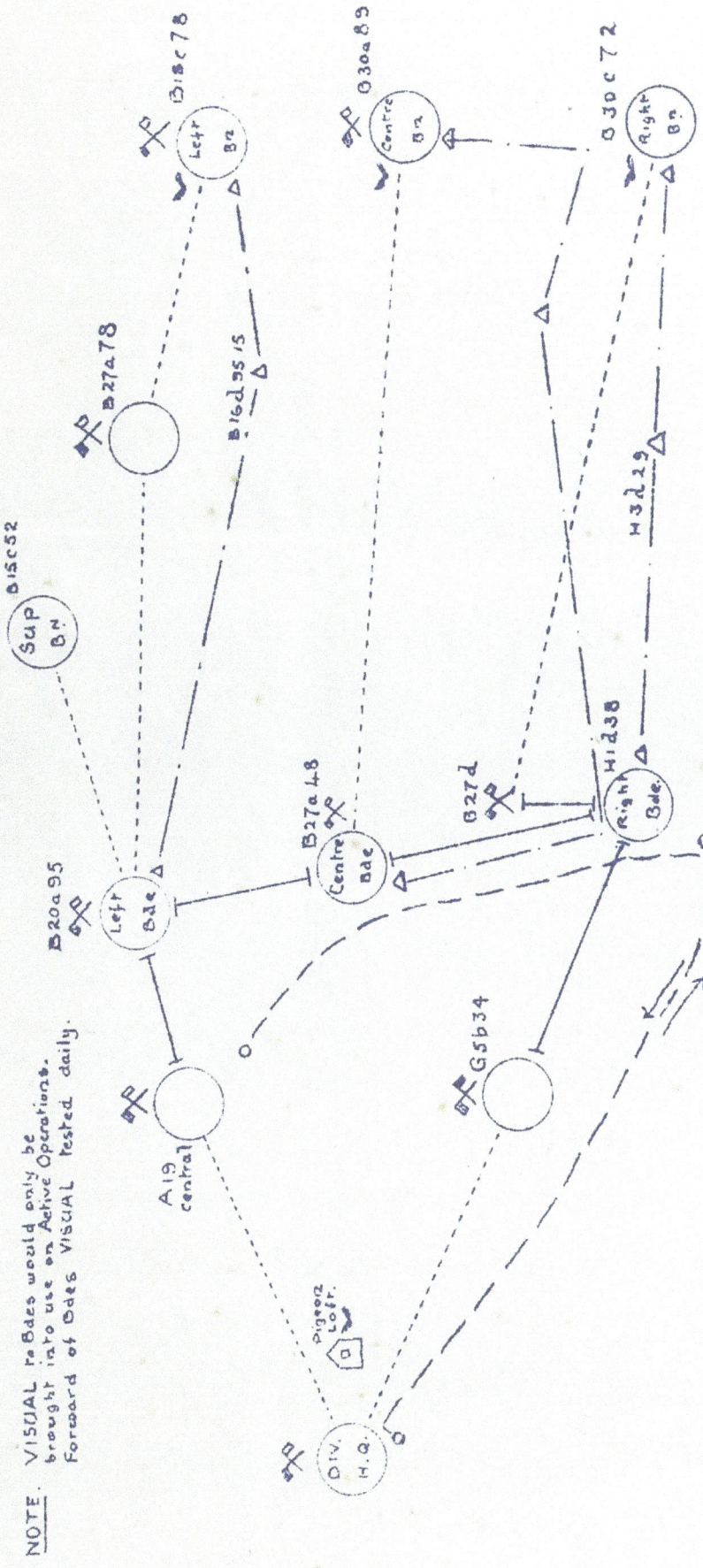

VISUAL, D.R.L.S., PIGEONS, RUNNER POSTS.

KEY.

△ = Runner Post
O = D.R.L.S. Post
⚑ = Visual Post

DRLS route = — — —
Runner " = —·—·—
Visual " = ·······
Telephone·· = ———

Nº 3.

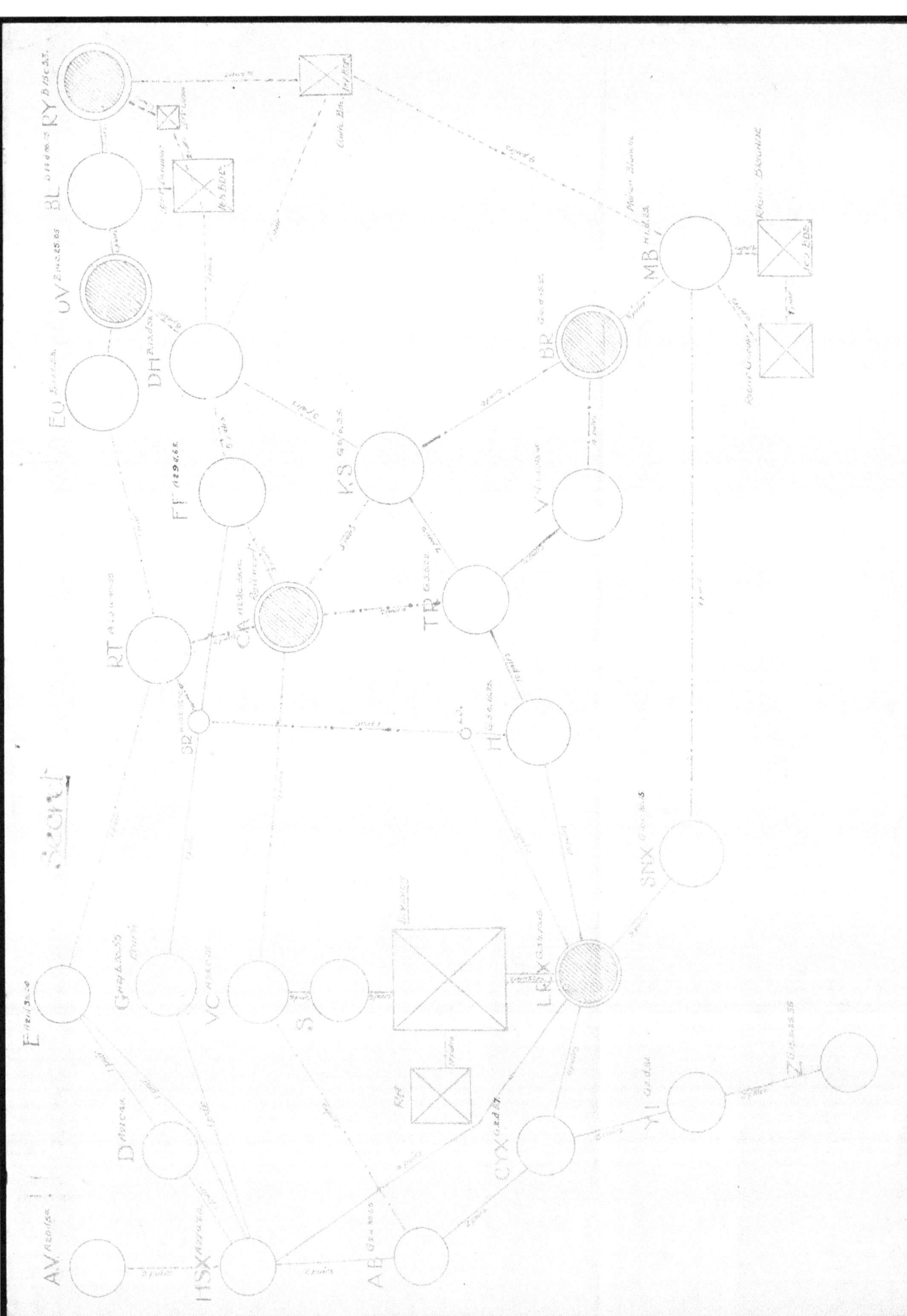

56th Div.

WAR DIARY

56th DIVISIONAL SIGNAL COMPANY, R.E.

M A R C H

1 9 1 8

Instructions regarding War Diaries and Intelligence
Summaries are contained in F. S. Regs., Part II.
and the Staff Manual respectively. Title pages
will be prepared in manuscript.

INTELLIGENCE SUMMARY.

(Erase heading not required.)

56th Divisional Signal Co RE

Place	Date	Hour	Summary of Events and Information	Remarks and references to Appendices
Victory Camp	1.3.18		Work on buried routes continued	G.K.
Roclincourt	2.3.18		Visual stations commenced at Left Centre & Right Bdes being established	G.K.
Victor Camp	3.3.18		Work on buried routes & visual stations continued	G.K.
"	4.3.18		As above	G.K.
"	5.3.18		As above	G.K.
"			Putting in buried test stations & digging parties for Buried Cable	G.K.
"			Lt. F.W. Clerk returned from leave	G.K.
"	6.3.18		Conference on Communications at XIII Corps H.Q.	G.K.
"			Buried routes continued	G.K.
"	6.3.18		Night digging parties commenced work on Left Bde buries	G.K.
"	7.3.18		Forward Communication scheme as above continued	G.K.
"	8.3.18		As above	G.K.
"	9.3.18		As above	G.K.
"	10.3.18		As above	G.K.
"	11.3.18		As above Left Bde Buried system put through in working condition	G.K.
"	12.3.18		Buried routes & test dugouts	G.K.
"	13.3.18		As above	G.K.
"	14.3.18		As above	G.K.
"	15.3.18		" above	G.K.
"	16.3.18		As above	G.K.

Gordon Kennard
Major RE
O C Signals 56 Division

Instructions regarding War Diaries and Intelligence Summaries are contained in F.S. Regs, Part II. and the Staff Manual respectively. Title Pages will be prepared in manuscript.

INTELLIGENCE SUMMARY

(Erase heading not required.)

56 Divisional Signal Coy RE

Place	Date	Hour	Summary of Events and Information	Remarks and references to Appendices
VICTORY CAMP	17.3.18		Work on Purried Routes Visual Stations + Wireless Dugouts continued	GK
ROCKINCOURT			All horses + transport moved to open country. Through enemy shelling	GK
	18.3.18		Signal office Div HQ moved to LRX dugout 200 yds N of Div HQ	GK
			All working parties working forward on R.E. Communications + buries	GK
"	19.3.18		Horses + Transport returned to Div HQ (original lines)	GK
"	20.3.18		Situation normal	GK
"	21.3.18		Situation normal	GK
"	22.3.18		Communications by buried cable routs from Div to Posts in front line put through	GK
			Company stood to 5 AM in expectation of enemies attack	GK
	23.3.18		As above	GK
	24.3.18		As above	GK
	25.3.18		As above	GK

G Kennard
Major RE
OC Signals 56 Div

INTELLIGENCE SUMMARY

(Erase heading not required.)

56 Divisional Signal Coy R.E.

Place	Date	Hour	Summary of Events and Information	Remarks and references to Appendices
VICTORY CAMP	26/3/18		Situation normal	G.R.
ROCKINCOURT	27/3/18		Situation normal	G.R.
"	28/3/18		Enemy attacked along whole 9 Divisional Front	G.R.
			167 Bde moved up in close support	G.R.
			All lines maintained & communication good	G.R.
"	29/3/18		Drivers & transport moved by route march to AGNIERES	G.R.
			Attacks again renewed all the afternoon	
			all beaten off with heavy losses to enemy	G.R.
			3RD CANADIAN Div signal officers visited area to take over	G.R.
"	29/3/18		DIV HQ moved to ACQ	G.R.
"	30/3/18		Relief completed by 3RD CAN DIV	G.R.
ACK	31/3/18		LINEMAN returned from Advanced Test points	G.R.
			Transport rejoined Company at ACK	G.R.

G. Kennard Major R.E.
O.C. Sigs 56 Div

56th Divisional Engineers

56th DIVISIONAL SIGNAL COMPANY R. E.

APRIL 1918.

Army Form C. 2118

WAR DIARY
or
INTELLIGENCE SUMMARY
(Erase heading not required.)

56 Divisional Signal Coy RE

Vol 27

Place	Date	Hour	Summary of Events and Information	Remarks and references to Appendices
H.T. ACQ	1.4.18		Overhauling stores & technical equipment	GK
"	2.4.18		Overhauling stores & company training	GK
"	3.4.18		As above	GK
"	4.4.18		As above + running stores	GK
"	5.4.18		As above	GK
"	6.4.18		Units of Canadian Div Area to relief by ourselves	GK
"	6.4.18		Advance party left by lorry that afternoon	GK
WARLUS	7.4.18	11.30 AM	Company moved by route march arriving WARLUS	GK
WARLUS	8.4.18		Communication established by cable. Visual wireless etc	GK
WARLUS	9.4.18		Overhauling routes & commencement of new buried routes in the Forward Area	GK
WARLUS	10.4.18		As above	GK
WARLUS	11.4.18		Buried cable route completed to TELEGRAPH HILL & RIGHT BAT HQ	GK
WARLUS	12.4.18		As above	GK

Gordon Kennard
Major RE
OC Signals 56 Division

Army Form C. 2118

WAR DIARY
or
INTELLIGENCE SUMMARY
(Erase heading not required.)

56 Divisional Signal Coy RE

Instructions regarding War Diaries and Intelligence Summaries are contained in F. S. Regs., Part II. and the Staff Manual respectively. Title Pages will be prepared in manuscript.

Place	Date	Hour	Summary of Events and Information	Remarks and references to Appendices
WARLUS	13.4.18		Diagram of Communications A. to 3 Bdes + artillery attached	G.K
WARLUS	14.4.18		Rear buried cable route from O to MS Right Reserve Bde front completed	G.K
WARLUS	15.4.18		G Dugout + new Bury therefrom commenced	G.K
	16.4.18		Work on Buried routes continued	G.K
"	17.4.18		As above	G.K
"	18.4.18		As above	G.K
"	19.4.18		As above	G.K
"	20.4.18		No 33 Area detachment 1 officer 8 O.R. reported	G.K
"	20.4.18		180 men working on T + G Buries	G.K
"			40 DAC commenced Artillery Bury	G.K
"	21.4.18		Lt Doust G reported for duty from 1st Army	G.K
"	22.4.18		Working on Buries + clearing area	G.K
"	23.4.18		40 Artillery working on new bury	G.K
"			Wireless school for Artillery commences	G.C
"			2nd Lieut G A Walker left for 1st Army Wireless section	G.K

Gordon Kennard
Major RE
OC Signals 56 Division

Army Form C. 2118

WAR DIARY
or
INTELLIGENCE SUMMARY
(Erase heading not required.)

56 Divisional Signal Coy RE

Place	Date	Hour	Summary of Events and Information	Remarks and references to Appendices
WARLUS	24.4.18		Took over from 15th Div taking over left sector.	O.K.
WARLUS	24.4.18		HQ Shelled Signal office transferred to cellar, communications maintained by mains ground cable already laid & everything O.K.	O.K.
WARLUS	25.4.18		Work on Buried Routes & Test Boxes in new area. Working party obtained from 167 Bde & burying commenced to Left Bat HQ	O.K.
WARLUS	26.4.18		As above Diagram of Communications marked B attached	O.K.
WARLUS	27.4.18		As above	O.K.
			5 Reinforcements for No 5 Sec Div HQ arrived	O.K.
WARLUS	28.4.18		Work on Buried routes & forward communications	O.K.
WARLUS	29.4.18		3 Reinforcements for No 5 section	O.K.
WARLUS	30.4.18		New bury to Left Bat Right Bde taped out	O.K.

G Kinnear Major RE
OC Signals
56 Division

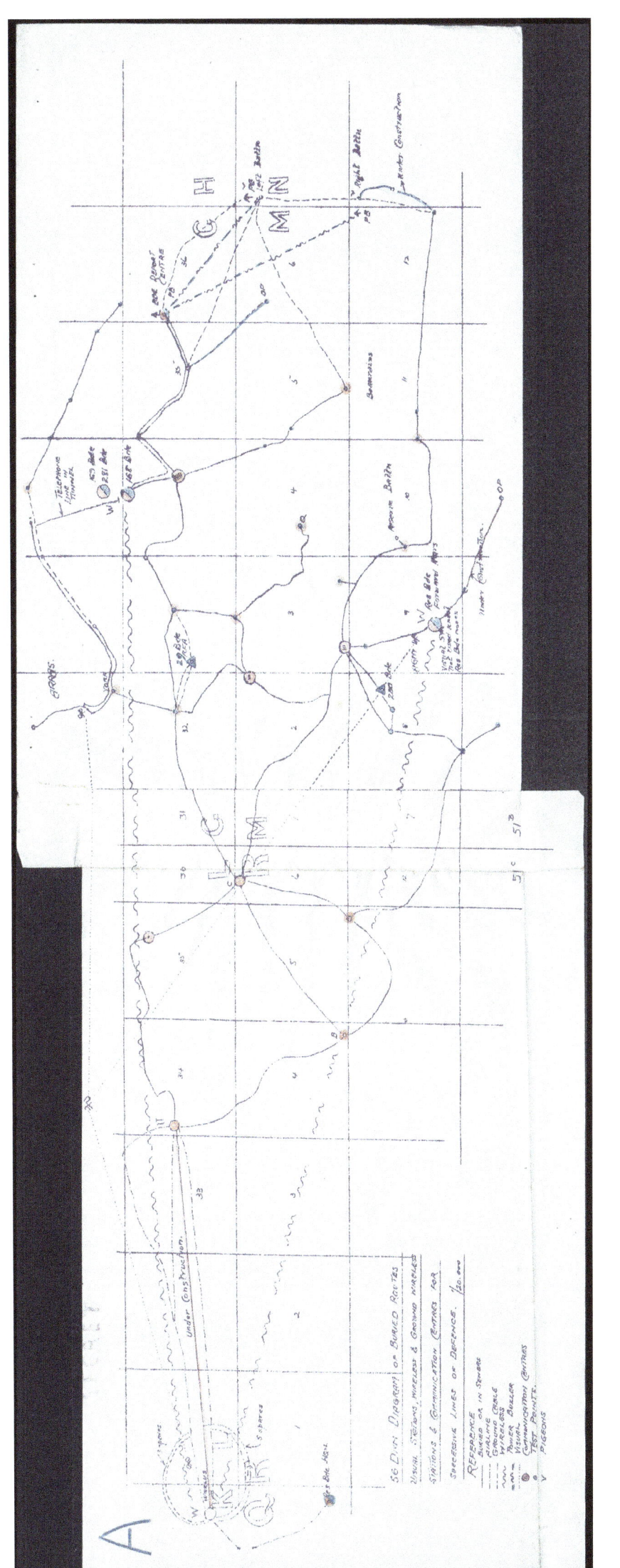

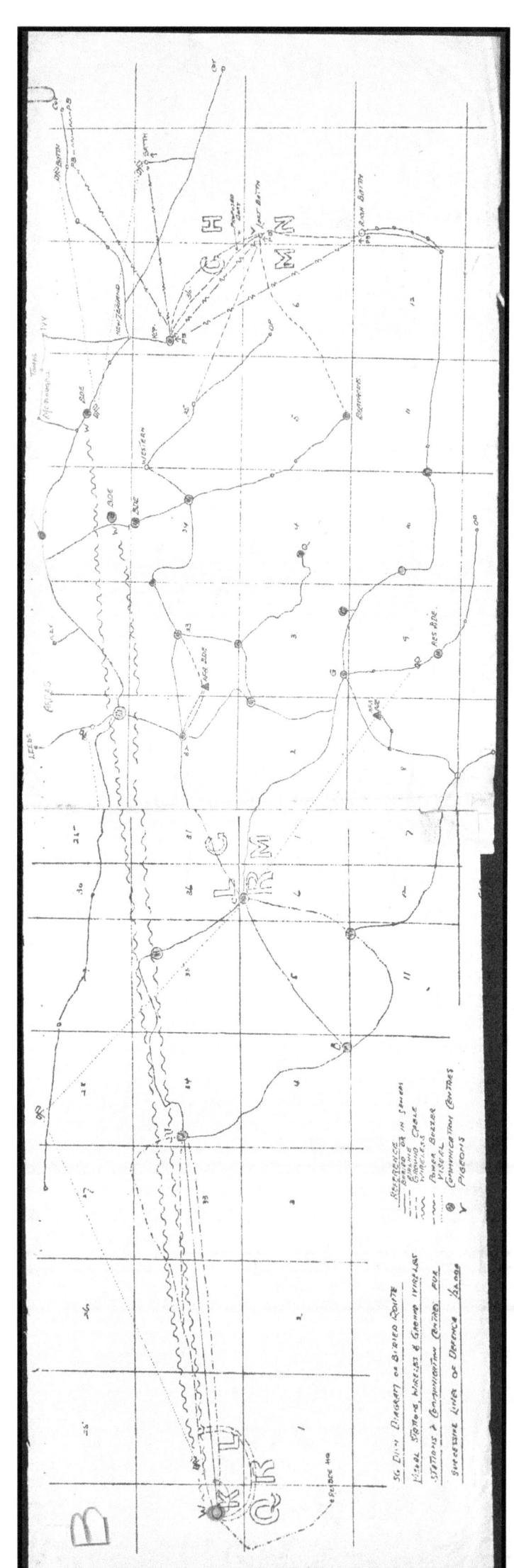

WAR DIARY
INTELLIGENCE SUMMARY

56D Signals
May
Vol 28

Army Form C. 2118

Place	Date	Hour	Summary of Events and Information	Remarks and references to Appendices
WARLUS	1/5/18		Work on buried system.	
"	2/5/18		As above.	
"	3/5/18		As above. Divisional front extended to the left. Necessary arrangements made.	
"	4/5/18		Work on buried system.	
"	5/5/18		As above. Work with R.E. lens on local wire.	
"	6/5/18		As above. 2/Lt. S.O. Marsdell to hospital sick.	
"	7/5/18		As above. 2/Lt. J.H. Ward to 281 Bde F.A. wire-wagon vice 2/Lt. Marsdell.	
"	8/5/18		As above. S.W. cable reeled up. Danville lines connected to it & my try by means of a buried system.	
"			& 14 pairs	
"	9/4/18		Capt. H.J.P. Hallo O.C. 215 Coy for handed over reported to H.Q. vice Capt. Lorhay in command. Work continued on buried system. Staff of Divisional wards of Chatham and General. Necessary arrangements have	
"	10/5/18		As above. Lt. C.E. Lucadores reported for duty with 281 Inf.-wires.	
"	11/5/18		As above. Capt D Rectoring left for 2nd Army Signal School.	
"	12/5/18		As above.	
"	13/5/18		As above.	
"	14/5/18		As above. 2/Lt. S.O. Marsdell reported 281 Bde, R.F.A.	
"	15/5/18		As above. 2/Lt. J.H. Ward returned to Division from 281 Bde.	
"	16/5/18		As above. 2 Officers (Lieut. R.F.) and 63 O.R. from infantry. Gunners and volunteer sun units reported for 3 weeks signal course. Completion for transport personal had.	
"	17/5/18		All available men working in parties, digging cables between the Grand and to complete lines to BERNEVILLE from WARLUS, the whole fact being fabricated to consist of 1 pt. of 4 pair, 6 pt. 17 pair, two	
"			completed in 4 hour per man.	
"	18/5/18			

WAR DIARY
or
INTELLIGENCE SUMMARY

(Erase heading not required.)

Army Form C. 2118

Instructions regarding War Diaries and Intelligence Summaries are contained in F.S. Regs., Part II. and the Staff Manual respectively. Title Pages will be prepared in manuscript.

Place	Date	Hour	Summary of Events and Information	Remarks and references to Appendices
WARLUS	19/4/18		Work on burial options, head lines rearranged, so as to get them underground as much as possible and to disturb by bombs instead of direct wire. (See diagram attached.)	App
"	20/4/18		As above. Work commenced on "B" dugout (near DAINVILLE STATION) (Much rails recovered)	App
"	21/4/18		Telephone connection completed throughout area for 24 hours. Battle of Traffic handled by Telegraph. Wires not much used.	App
			Construction of new dugout on X-13 route at R.4.a.55 (record 3.R) commenced	
			Work on local system & "B" dugout continued	
"	22/4/18		Work as above continued. Overhauling of X-C and X-13 route commenced	App
"	23/4/18		As above	App X
"	24/4/18		As above. New lines constructed to left Bn. Bt. Hd. (T.V) from point on RP-LB buy (T.J) stations by D.R. D-v.s or Normantsburg	"
"	25/4/18		As above. Work commenced on protection of HS. station against enemy.	App
"	26/4/18		As above continued	
"	27/4/18		As above. Major G.C. Kennard M.C. to hospital sick. Capt. H.J.P. Mallett assumed Temporary command	App
"	28/4/18		Parties wire parties in out of Capture Jewel & Juchin wires to installation of ground return	App
"	29/4/18		Inspection of transport by C.R.E.	App
"	30/4/18		Nets on house	App
"	24/4/18		Work or train. New lead system, ext. D.R. dugout finished	App

m.p Mallett Capt
acty OC signals 56 th Division (T.F.)

LOCAL SYSTEM

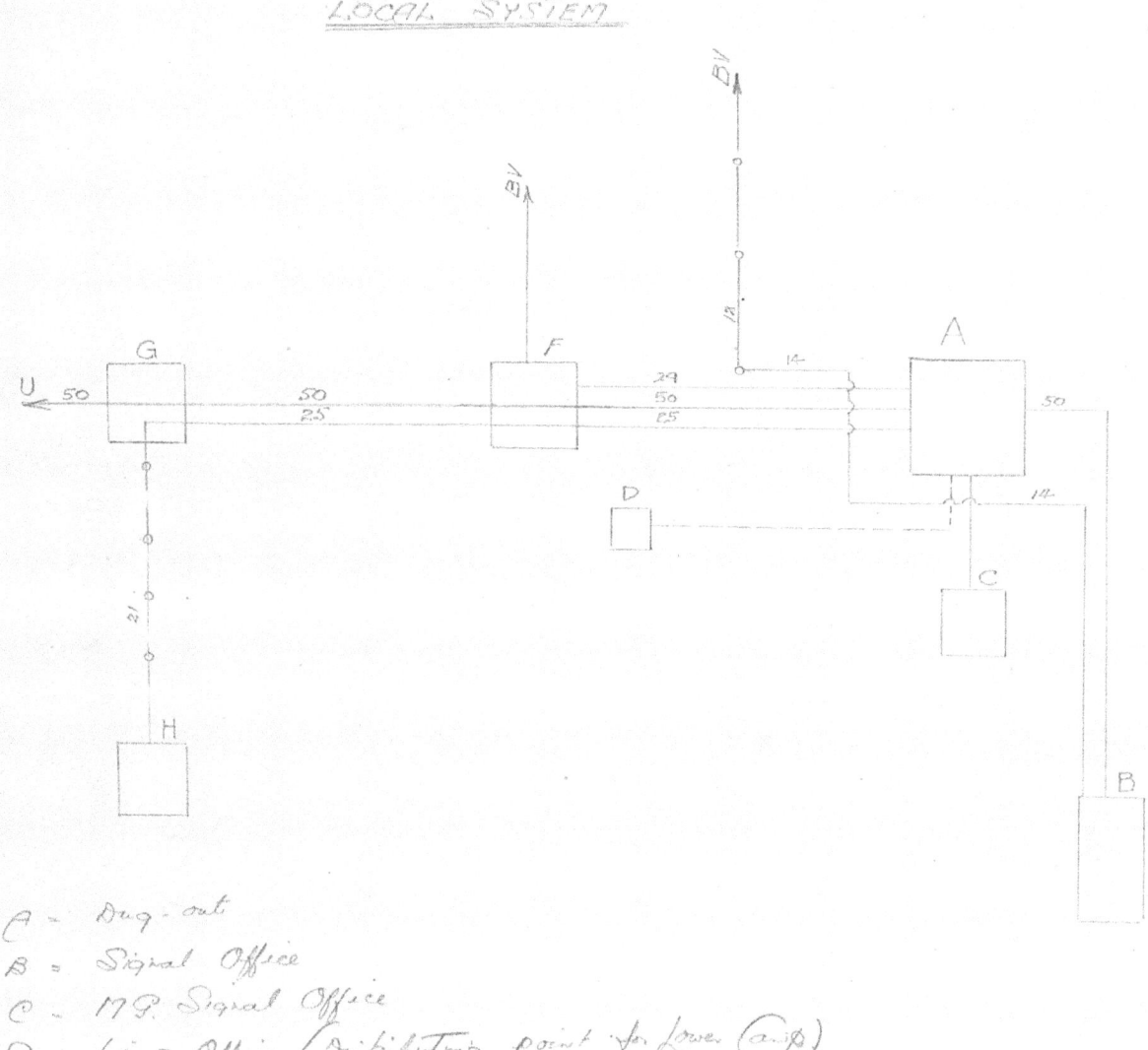

A = Dug-out
B = Signal Office
C = M.G. Signal Office
D = Lines Office (Distributing point for Lower Camp)
E = Permanent Pole (G.P.S.)
F = Junction for BV bury
G = Box for Upper Camp
H = M.G. Billet (Distributing point for Upper Camp).

WAR DIARY or INTELLIGENCE SUMMARY

Army Form C. 2118

56 D Signals

Vol 29

Month and year: **JUNE 1918**

Place	Date	Hour	Summary of Events and Information	Remarks and references to Appendices
WARLUS	1/VI/18		Work on "B" dugout continued. Strengthening of "J" dugout begun. Miscellaneous work in town.	nil
"	2/VI/18		Church Parade 20.0's killed by shell hit on F.A. O.P. 51 G.S.W. N7a 30.70.	nil
"	3/VI/18		Work as on 1st. 4 C.A.K. exchanges changed at midnight.	nil
"	4/VI/18		Work on above "B" dugout finished, and transfer of lines commenced. B8 and X2 routes returned, where required by early day trenches. "J" dugout continued.	nil
"	5/VI/18		Work in above and adversary. J-H route. When enemy in afternoon.	nil
"	6th		Capt (A/Major) A.J. RANSFORD R.E. assumed command of Company. Vice Capt (A/Major) G.C. KENNARD RE(T) evacuated sick on 26th ult. Telegraphists and Telephonists par in front of Corps Hq. 80 messages sent by visual and 53 by wireless. Work continued on B and J test points.	A/c. A/g. A/g.
"	7th		"	A/g
"	8th		Work as yesterday. 167th Inf. Bde relieved 168 Inf Bde in left sector. Church parade	
"	9th			
"	10th		One party commenced dismantling NEW ZEALAND test point G 20 c 20.25 (CAMBRAI ROAD) and moving it to a deeper cellar. Present cellar cracked by shell. B point finished on 8th. J point continues.	A/g A/g
"	11th		nil	A/g
"	12th		BV Cable Section (17th Corps) commenced burying the D-YORK route, where it is exposed by newly dug trenches. Work on NEW ZEALAND and J-Q route continued. O-N3 Burg broken by shell fire late at night.	A/g
"	13th		One party repaired ONS bury at M15 b.8.8 and filled shell holes. One party on the JQ route, and BV Cable Sect. on YORK-D. DC and DH routes.	A/g

WAR DIARY or INTELLIGENCE SUMMARY.

Army Form C. 2118.

JUNE 1918 Sheet 2.

Place	Date	Hour	Summary of Events and Information	Remarks and references to Appendices
WAILLY	14/6/18		Work as yesterday. Party which yesterday repaired ONE bury today continued to bury up exposed portions of the YC route.	ML
"	15th		New Zealand test point finished. DH and HN routes finishes by BV Cable test, and HQ route commenced. JQ route finished.	ML
"	16th		Church parade.	ML
"	17th		Work on YC and GH routes. BV Cable test on the GC route. 8 patrols.	ML
"			Commenced work on a new tel Dugout for O at Mq.d.1.2. HQ/JBBe Wge2/344 Be in offices.	ML
"	18th		OHP and CAN Rist opi path by the R. Scarpe fixed up to Lieff B2e Relays.	ML
"			One bury YC and GC route under repair. Removal of PA test point SK16.	ML
"	19th		9P (MHQ 5.0) King Sthos out with terminal strips. Ex route tested out.	ML
"	20th		9P (point finished) One party on repairing the PB-T bury (cut by working party)	ML
"	21st		Ex route tested out	ML
"	22nd		Transport and harness inspection.	ML
"	23rd		Capt H.P. HALLETT left for GHQ. Lieut ALDRIDGE l/t for CONDETTE on 3 week	ML
"			bicycle (Signal/Tel) course. Church parade. Working party of 170 men	ML
"	24th	(OW)	London fought Bug 200 yards to fore Dugs. Wire buried 2 ft deep.	ML
"			Route & Guy Wires LT poles at G.3.a.d 85.65 to the new battalion Headqrs at	

WAR DIARY or INTELLIGENCE SUMMARY

Army Form C. 2118.

Sheet 3

JUNE 1918

Place	Date	Hour	Summary of Events and Information	Remarks and references to Appendices
WIRLESS	23/6/18 cont.		H.25 to 15.00 off London Avenue, with a spur to the new Support Battalion Hqrs at H.25 a 9.2. Bury to contain 3 7pair brass cables - 21 pairs.	A2
	24.		The 8 pioneers who completed O point on the 23rd inst. commenced a similar dugout at P (M10 C 15.95) today. One party put through the cables in TP point and sandbagged the front in the trench at M9 C 7.5. One party on the O.C. route laying D point with plugs and sockets, and commenced H point. Bury continued and one way front on the ARRAS-DOULLENS road. By Cable Sect completed 24 110 yards of the 2nd tandems (R.F.)	A2
"	25.		Parties on O.C. route 300 yards bury completed and filled in.	A2
"	26.		Parties on O.C. and Y. By Sect on H point. 170 men 7th Middlesex continue bury. 169 M Rec relieved 167 H/ Bn in left sector.	A2
"	27.		New Jones P.U.O. commenced - 11 cases in the company. Bury continued by 7th Middlesex	A2
"	28.		P.U.O. now 1 officer 90 OR. 7th Middlesex (2 coys) continues bury.	A2
"	29.		P.U.O. now 3 officers 32 OR. 1 coy 7th Middlesex finished bury on left sector.	A2
"	30.		Special Church Service commemorating 1st July 1916 - commencement of Somme offensive.	A2

M Rainford Major RE
OC 56th (7th London) Div Sig Co RE
30/6/18

H.Q. "A",
   56th. Division.

   Reference AX 368 of the 8th. inst. I attach herewith War Diary for July for 56th. Divisional Signal Co. R.E.   War Diaries for other units under my command have already been sent to A.G's. office at the base.   I will arrange for them to be sent to your office in future.

8/8/18.

                                    Lieut. Col. R.E.
                              C.R.E. 56th. Division.

"A" Form
AND SIGNALS.

Army Form C. 2121
(in pads of 100).

No. of Message............

rds	Charge	This message is on a/c of :	Recd. at........m.
Sent ....m.		................Service	Date.............
		(Signature of "Franking Officer")	From............ By.............

y of Month	In reply to Number	AAA
10	E 898/95	
	draw	from
	forward	
	7500	
	300	medium
	200	M.& Port
		roll
	for	3x2
	heavy	Defa
	and	Neulo
	and	s
4	sheet	C
4	sheet	Steel

rected. (Z)

Page 1

Army Form C. 2118.

WAR DIARY
or
INTELLIGENCE SUMMARY.
(Erase heading not required.)

JULY 1918.

56th DIVL SIGNAL COY. R.E.

Place	Date	Hour	Summary of Events and Information	Remarks and references to Appendices
WARLUS	1st		Work on O test point at M9d.2.1, and Y test point at L35b.1.4 continued. P test point completed and buried.	Sheet 51 b+c 1/40000 MP
	2nd		2/Lieut Burgess R.G.A. reports from 19th Bde R.G.A. for 1 months attachment. Lieut (A/Capt) D.W. Aldridge posted 2IC in command of Company. Party commenced work on the G.C. Route repairing the route at frequent exchanges.	MP.
	3rd		Nil	MP.
	4th		Two coys 5th Monmouthshire commenced burying open TW test point at M6b.9.8 to the new Battalion HQrs in North Alley Switch at M6d.9.7, under supervision of 2/Lieut Burgess and 2/Lieut Heavey.	MP.
	5th		Work on Y, P, K test points. New Signal Office hut on top of dugout completed. No working party tonight.	MP.
	6th		Signal Office moved from Bétonmont on Wanquetin Road to the new hut. 2/Lieut Burgess supervised extension of bury. 2/Lieut Thomson and Heath 10ans. 310 yards.	MP.
	7th		Bury continued under 2/Lieut Thomson and Heath 10ans. 310 yards. Cable to 6 feet.	MP.
	8th		Division to be relieved on the 15th inst. Work on P and K continued. 2/Lieut ___ in charge of buried cable work.	MP.

Page 2.

Army Form C. 2118.

WAR DIARY
INTELLIGENCE SUMMARY

JULY 1918
56th Divl. Signal Coy. R.E.

Place	Date	Hour	Summary of Events and Information	Remarks and references to Appendices
WARLUS	9th		Orders for relief by 2nd Canadian Divn. at 10 am 15th Inf. Bde received on relief 167 Bde to go to MANIN 168 Bde to LIGNEREUIL 169 Bde to IZEL LEZ-HAMEAU. Lieut. E.H. COE R.E. reported for duty and posted to 167 Inf. Bde. Vice Lieut (A/Capt) ALDRIDGE. Buzzer ctd. Forward by field Buzzer.	AN.
	10th		Work on K and P continued. Busy cont. work on Wireless Telephone on lorry.	A/6
	11th		Buzz continued by London Scottish under Lieut. Leary and Armstrong. DC Signals 2nd Can. Divn. arrived to look round area	A/6
	12th		Sent over first load of signals to LE CAUROY Sig. HQ at 10 am 15th Inf. Bde. relieved at dark	A/6
	13th		G.O.C. inspected Horses harness and waggons. K and P pants ctd completed. 168 Bde moved to AVESNES-LE-COMTE Area	A/6
			Lines arranged for Brigade in rest area. Two lorries loaded, J. SVc. sent to LE CAUROY. Move to LE CAUROY cancelled at 9.30 pm	M.2
	14th		Divl HQ Open at ROELLECOURT at 10 am. Harbourers 167 Bde sig. moved to BERNEVILLE after relief 168 Bde moved from AVESNES ditto to LIGNEREUIL ditto.	A/2

WAR DIARY
or
INTELLIGENCE SUMMARY.

(Erase heading not required.)

Page 3   JULY 1918.

56th Divl. Signal Coy. R.E.

Army Form C. 2118.

Place	Date	Hour	Summary of Events and Information	Remarks and references to Appendices
ROELLECOURT	15th	6pm	Company marched off from WARLUS at 7.30 am this morning and arrived here at 5pm. 167 Bde moved to ORLENCOURT & Superimposed sounder and telephone out. Furnished D8 cable. 168 Bde moved from LIGNEREUIL to CHELERS area. Superimposed sounder and telephone. 169 Bde from LIGNY to DIEVAL. Sounder and phone direct. Visual local LINES TAKEN UP. connected up.	AW
	16th		H.Q. Batln moved to MAGNICOURT EN COMTE. Wireless section Scheme by D.R. Cas. Stn. 107 Sect. arrived at ROELLECOURT	AW
	17th		Orders issued to move to VILLERS CHATEL 10am tomorrow	AW
VILLERS CHATEL	18th		Opened office 10am at VILLERS CHATEL 167 Bde moved to VILLERS BRULIN, direct pair phone and phone. 169 Bde moved at DIEVAL Noble end phone via 17th Corps at BRYAS. 168 Bde moved to CAMP DE LA HAIE, visual and phone via 8th Corps at CAMBLAIN L'ABBÉ and 20th Divn at CHAM DE LA HAIE	AW
	19th		Cable laid from BRUIS to LA COMTE to connect one to 169 Bde Cable hut by Visual Signalling established to 168 and 169 Bdes. GHQ exchange to from ESTREE CAUCHIE to GAUCHIN L'ÉGAL	AW

Page 4.

WAR DIARY
or
INTELLIGENCE SUMMARY.
(Erase heading not required.)

56th Divl. Signal Coy. R.E.T.   JULY 1918   Army Form C. 2118.

Place	Date	Hour	Summary of Events and Information	Remarks and references to Appendices
VILLERS CHATEL	19th		(Continued) to complete line to 56th M.G. Battn. Visual worked to 168 and 169 Bdes from 8am to Noon	AM.
	20th			
	21st		In addition to visual as above, loop wireless worked from R.w. to 167 Bde at VILLERS BRULIN. 20 line S.C. exchange brand returned to G.H.Q. Army and 40 line D.C. exchange drawn in its place. Staff cutter drawn from Divl. dump at WAVRANS. Signal School assembled.	AM.
	22nd		R.A. H.Q.S. moved from WARLUS to AUBIGNY Chau. Signal School commenced. Two men per Brigade Section reports for loop wireless course. 10 men sent to 1st Army Rest Camp near BOULOGNE for 14 days.	M.G.
	23rd		Cable laid from BAJUS to 169 Bde at DIEVAL for CRE and as cable to LA COMTE picked up.	M.G.
	24th		Visual practice as usual. 3 Signallers per Battn. reports for Power Buzzer instruction. 2 Signallers per Battn. in addition reports to their respective Brigade Sections for Power Buzzer work.	AM.
	25th		Communication schemes all day. Cable wagons & wireless section. Brazier and visual used.	M.G.
	26th		169 Bde visual scheme – worked well. Picking up of Lucas aides by use of smoke candle.	M.G.

Army Form C. 2118.

WAR DIARY
or
INTELLIGENCE SUMMARY.
(Erase heading not required.)

Page 5.

JULY 1918

55th DIVL. SIGNAL COY. R.E.

Place	Date	Hour	Summary of Events and Information	Remarks and references to Appendices
VILLERS CHATEL	27th		Experimented with various Smoke Signals for use with visual. GRENADE No 27 or 37, Phosphorus, Hand and Rifle appears to be the best.	M.
	28th		Poplar Panel Practice – 167 Bde.	M.
	29th		2/Lieut BURGESS returned to the 19th Bde R.C.A. on completion of his attachment. LIEUT DAW S.E. 1/7th Middlesex Regt attached for duty under Divisional arrangement.	M.
			Company run 2nd in Buckhampton Race and 3rd in Bumping Competition at the CREi Sports.	Apx.
	30th		17th Corps moved from KRYAC to DUISANS 10am The morning. Orders received to relieve 1st Can. Div. at 10am August 2nd Div MQ to be at WARLUS and not at ETRUN where 1st Can Div MQ are.	M.
	31st		Visual scheme. All wireless stores sent to WARLUS and station of Right Bde relieved.	M.

A. Ransford
MAJOR.
COMMANDING 55th DIVISIONAL SIGNAL COY. R.E.

Army Form C. 2118.

WAR DIARY
or
INTELLIGENCE SUMMARY.
(Erase heading not required.)

56th DIVL. SIGNAL COY. R.E. T. VOL 31

AUGUST 1918.

Instructions regarding War Diaries and Intelligence Summaries are contained in F.S. Regs., Part II. and the Staff Manual respectively. Title pages will be prepared in manuscript.

Place	Date	Hour	Summary of Events and Information	Remarks and references to Appendices
VILLERS CHATEL	1st		Linesmen for Buried cable test points, motorcyclist stores and instruments and 8m 2 Steel sent to WARLUS. CAPT. ALDRIDGE, LIEUT McIVOR	
			DOUST and 2 Lieut McIVOR sent to WARLUS to take over and arrange for switch lines at 10 am tomorrow.	
WARLUS	2nd		Company marched at 9 am and arrives here at 12.30 p.m. Party of about 30 men went by light Railway. Billets in WARLUS still occupied by Canadians. 167 Bde Hqrs. & of AGNY at M14 a 3.7. M.	
			168 Bde at RUE PASTEUR, ARRAS. 169 Bde at RUE JEANNE D'ARC, ARRAS M.	
			167 (Right) Bde Have one battalion in line 169 (Centre) Bde Have two Battalions in line and 168 (Left) Bde have one Battalion in line. Covering artillery 280 and 281 2nd Bdes RFA	
			282 Army RFA Bde and 180th Bde RFA (16th Div)	
			Visual stations chosen. Terminals at YEF R1a 2.9. ARRAS CITADEL (for left and Centre Bde) which are connected to station by phone. G 26 d 2.0 AGNY (for 167 Bde) M14 a 3.7. Transmitting Station at R11 a 6.5 near WAILLY WOOD. Arranged with 167 Bde to dig a trench down F. pond (M2c 7.0) to C2 p 2.4	
	3rd			

WAR DIARY
INTELLIGENCE SUMMARY

Page 2. AUGUST 1918. 56th. Divl. Signal Coy. R.E. T.

Army Form C. 2118.

(Erase heading not required.)

Place	Date	Hour	Summary of Events and Information	Remarks and references to Appendices
WARLUS	3rd (continued)		at M.14.a.37. 100 pairs (4 25 pair paper cables) 10 V.B. buried in over to exit out of F. park. Another installed at the following (a) points: U.C.K.L.H.G. Cz (167 Bde). FV (169 Bde). NZ (168 Bde.) one each. Also one man temporarily at York, WIGAN. Power Buzzer and Amplifier now installed at Line Batt. and in the Right Bde. Left Batt. Centre Bde Line Battn. Left Bde and KP. Left Bde Withdraws one battalion to Reserve.	Nil
	4th		Working parties clearing up cables left by Canadian. T.T. Cable section working on F-CZ being.	Nil
	5th			Nil
	6th		With as yesterday.	Nil
	7th		Parties laying up WARLUS and BERNEVILLE. Power Buzzer and Amplifier withdrawn from Right Brigade Report Centre to Right Brigade Hqrs. Material for new test point (PC) on PT. buried at M.12.C.25.75, sent out in G.S. Wagon. G.S. Wagon on way home. 4 horses killed. Two Drivers killed, one wounded	Nil

WAR DIARY

AUGUST 1918.

Page 3

56TH SIGNAL COY RE (T)

Army Form C. 2118.

Place	Date	Hour	Summary of Events and Information	Remarks and references to Appendices
WARLUS	8th		Third heavy spark working on the T-TH bury.	Nil.
	9th		T-TH bury now OK. Trouble caused by cables being fused by cables in T. dugout. Parties cleaned up Berneville and Dainville.	Nil.
	10th		Work as yesterday.	Nil.
	11th		Arranged with C.E. XVII Corps, O.C. 2nd Can. Works Bn. and AD Sigs. to commence burying cable tomorrow night on Tuesday night.	Nil.
	12th		Tapes out bury from PC to Batt. 119 at M12.c.25.75, and from Batt. Hqrs at M17.c.0.6 via Batt. Hqrs at M17.a.1.6 to PB at M11.c.5.9. TW-NA bury completed by 169 Bde. Cpl Page and party commenced rewiring NS test point. Lieut Boust proceeds on leave. NS continued. 400 men of 2nd Can. Works Bn. digging tonight.	Nil.
	13th		Last nights party failed to complete their task. NS completed. Warning that 15th Div. will relieve 56th Div. at 10am 18th inst.	Nil.
	14th			Nil.

WAR DIARY
INTELLIGENCE SUMMARY

Army Form C. 2118.

Page 4. AUGUST 1918.
56th DIVL. SIGNAL COY. R.E. T

Place	Date	Hour	Summary of Events and Information	Remarks and references to Appendices
WARLUS	15th		Signal School returned to units. Burys continued last night.	Nil.
	16th		167 Bde relieved and moved to IZEL-LES-HAMEAU at 6.30 pm. Informed by G.O.C. that Div will probably attack on TILLOY – TELEGRAPH HILL front through the 15th Div on 22nd inst. approx.	Nil.
	17th		2 NCO's and 4 men sent to ARRAS to fix up AUCKLAND CAVES as Adv. Div. Hqrs. Rear Div Hqrs. to be in TUNNEL, ARRAS moat. Selected visual stations on Cathedral and at Imperial for forthcoming operations.	Nil.
LE CAUROY	18th		Div Hqrs. closes WARLUS 10am, and opens LE CAUROY same hour. 168 Bde relieved and moved to MAIZIERES. Column marched off under "Field Inflow at 9am. Dismounted men went with Thomson by metre gage railway. 56th Div. Arty, moves to BERNEVILLE	Nil.

Army Form C. 2118.

WAR DIARY
or
INTELLIGENCE SUMMARY.
(Erase heading not required.)

Page 5. AUGUST 1918.
56th DIVL. SIGNAL COY R.E.T.

Place	Date	Hour	Summary of Events and Information	Remarks and references to Appendices
LE CAUROY	19th		169 Bde moved up to RUE ST. AUBERT ARRAS. YEFR opened in ARRAS, near the Fishmarket.	AIR
	20th		Cpl Page and 6 men sent up to ARRAS with instruments. Signal instructions for forthcoming operations in front of ARRAS, completed.	AIR
	21st		169 Bde moved back from ARRAS to AVESNES-LE-COMTE. 2/Lieut Heavey proceeds on leave. Transferred from XVII to VI Corps at 12.noon today. 167 Bde moved to BARLY, 168 to ST AMAND and 169 to SAULTY.	AIR
BAVINCOURT	22nd		Div. closed LE CAUROY 9am, opened BAVINCOURT Chateau same hour. 168 Bde moved to Sqd 6.2 - allotted three power Buzzer, one Power buzzer and amplifier, one loop set, 24 pigeons. AV. Div. Hqrs will close BAVINCOURT 10pm, and open BLAIREVILLE quarry same hour. Rear Hqrs remain at BAVINCOURT. Visual and wireless communication fixed up from Adv. Div. Hqrs to 168 Bde Hqrs.	AIR Sheet 51E

WAR DIARY

Army Form C. 2118.

Page 6.   AUGUST 1918
56th Divl. Signal Coy. R.E.T.

Place	Date	Hour	Summary of Events and Information	Remarks and references to Appendices
BLAIRVILLE	23rd		168 Bde attacked 4.55 am. All objectives gained. Rear Div. H.Q. moved from BAVINCOURT to BASSEUX at 11 am. Col Langley with one cable wagon and two limbers moved to BLAIRVILLE. 167 Bde relieved 168 Bde at Sq d 6.2. 169 Bde moved from SAULTY to BASSEUX.	NIL
	24th		168 Bde returned to BLAIRVILLE 167 Bde attacked at 7 am and gained all objectives. Power Buzzers and Amplifiers established at 167 Bde and Report centre. Two Power buzzers forward. Wilson set moved to Div. R.C. at S 2 d 0.4. Visual at BLAIRVILLE closed down and sent forward to Sgt. Morris at Sq d 6.2. New line laid from Sq d 6.2 to T 19 c central. 167 Bde moved to T 19 c central at 7 pm. Direct visual from S 1 d 7.0 to Bde. 169 Bde moved to Sq d 6.2. Div. Report centre moved from S 2 d 0.4 to Sq d 6.2. Renewing cable detachment. O.S.M. Bowden detachment. C&M wireless brought up to BLAIRVILLE. Div. Transferred from VI to XVII Corps. BV cable section attached.	NIL

WAR DIARY

Page 7. August 1918

56th Divl. Signal Coy RE (T)

Place	Date	Hour	Summary of Events and Information	Remarks and references to Appendices
BLAIREVILLE	25th		169 Bde moved at 8am to S11 d 8.0. 168 Bde moved to S9 d 6.2. Divl Report centre moved from S9 d 6.2 to S11 a 6.7. Two pairs laid from S tat point and one from BLAIREVILLE to new R.C. Forward lines to 167 and 169. Back lines to 168 and YEFR tied into new R.C.	AHL
	26th		167 Bde attacked in conjunction with 52nd Divn. and Canadian Corps on the left. 169 Bde moved to T14 c 9.0 and relieved 167 Bde. 168 moved to S11 d 8.0.	AHL
BOISLEUX-ST-MARC	27th		169 Bde moved again to T4 c 5.7 - Cpl Hockley extended line from T14 c 9.0. 168 Bde moved to T14 c 9.0. Adv. Div. Hqrs closed BLAIREVILLE and opened S11 a 6.7 (BOISLEUX-ST-MARC.) at 5 pm. Rear Hqrs moved to BLAIREVILLE same hour.	AHL

WAR DIARY
INTELLIGENCE SUMMARY

Page 8.   56th Divl. Signal Coy R.E. T.   AUGUST 1918   Army Form C. 2118.

Place	Date	Hour	Summary of Events and Information	Remarks and references to Appendices
BOISLEUX- ST. MARC.	28th		168 Bde moved to T.46 b.8.9. Working through 167 Bde temporarily. Col Langley laid new pair from YEPR to 168. Col Langley's detachment extended 169 Bde line to their new headquarters at T.U.7.d.0.8, under machine gun fire. 167 Bde took over two Battn. front E. of CROISILLES. 169 Bde attacked at NOON.	MR
	29th		169 Bde moved to U.7 d.0.8. 168 Bde moved to U.1 c.0.0 and then to U.7 d.7.4, without warning. 168 Bde line extended to U.7 d.7.4 by HUTTON. Both Bde lines dis several times owing to barrage on SENSEE VALLEY. Adv. Exchange established at T.22 a.1.7, and all lines led through it. Col Hockley laid a new pair from EFPC (T.22 a.1.7) to 169 Bde. 167 Bde closed at T.19 c central, moved to U.7.d.0.8 and relieved 168 and 169 Bdes. Visual established from T.23 a.2.7 to Brigades.	MR

WAR DIARY or INTELLIGENCE SUMMARY

Page 9.   August 1918   Army Form C. 2118.

56th DIVL. SIGNAL COY. R.E. (T)

Place	Date	Hour	Summary of Events and Information	Remarks and references to Appendices
BOISLEUX- ST-MARC.	30.		169 Bde Hqrs moved back to T.4 b.5.7. Directing Station moved from S11 a.6.7. to T.22 a.1.7. Trench cat borrowed from Corps and established at S11 a.6.7. 168 Bde Relieves 167 Bde in line.	A.M.
	31st.		169 Bde in Reserve Relieves by 155 Bde and moves to S.9 d.5.1. 167 Bde Relieves by 156 Bde and moves to T.19 c central. 168 Bde will be relieves tonight by 155 Bde tonight, and will move to T.14 c.9.0. Cables waiting for all Three Brigades. 168 Bde attacked this morning at 5.15 am. Station Redoubt captures. 52nd Div take over from 56th Div at T.22.a.1.7 early tomorrow morning. 56th Div Rear Hqrs closes at BLAIREVILLE 9am, and reopened S11 a.5.7. Same hour. 63rd Div has taken over BLAIREVILLE Hqrs.	Nil.

R. Ransford, MAJOR,
COMMANDING 56th DIVISIONAL SIGNAL COY. R.E.

WAR DIARY

INTELLIGENCE SUMMARY

(Erase heading not required.)

56th Divl. Signal Coy RE(T) SEPTEMBER 1918

Page 1

Army Form C. 2118.

Place	Date	Hour	Summary of Events and Information	Remarks and references to Appendices
BOISLEUX	1st		Division relieved by 52nd Divn. Command passed at 5am. 52nd	2/Lt/
ST. MARC			Divn Hqrs at T.22.a.1.7. Brigade Hqrs now as follows 167 Bde. S.13.	
S.14. 5.6.			T.19.c central. 168 Bde. T.14.c.9.0. 169 Bde. S.9.d.5.11.	Nil.
Sled S.18.				
	2nd		Nil.	Nil.
	3rd		Making up deficiencies in stores and overhauling equipment.	
	4th		Trench Buzzer sets sent to each Inf. Bde. with a pack animal	
			and saddle for transport. Power Buzzer etc personnel split	
			up and sent to Brigades. Received warning order that Divn.	Nil.
			will move to D.1.c.8.4. (QUÉANT) tomorrow with a view to	
			relieving 63rd Divn. the next day.	
	5th	9am	Arranged relief of 63rd Divn Signals and dumped accumulated	
			kit. Lieut ABRAHAM reported no. of NCOs sent 2/Lieut TICHMARSH supernumary.	Nil.
		3pm	Relief of 63rd Divn cancelled. Warning order received to relieve	
			1st Divn in XXII Corps in the near future.	
	6th		Division transferred to XXII Corps. 168 Bde moved to O.16.a.2.6. in	Nil.
			1st Divn area, in support. Communication via 1st Divn	

Page 2

WAR DIARY

INTELLIGENCE SUMMARY.

SEPTEMBER 1918. Army Form C. 2118.

56th SIGNAL COY. RE. (T)

Place	Date	Hour	Summary of Events and Information	Remarks and references to Appendices
BOISLEUX ST. MARC S11.a.5.5	7th		1 Officer, Visual Section and one cable section sent to LES FOSSES FARM (N.12.a.0.4) to commence take over from 1st Div Signals. 168 Bde Relieved Left Bde 1st Div in the line, Headquarters at P14.c.3.?	Sheet 51/13. MB.
	8th		169 Bde moved to O.16.a.4.5. Remainder of Company transport under 2/Lieut TITCHMARSH marched to FOSSES FARM. One office Relief sent to VA. 169 Bde relieved Right Bde 1st Div. HQ at P15.b.6.4. 167 Bde moved to ARRAS G.21.d.9.0 in XXII Corps Reserve.	MB.
FOSSES FARM N.12.a.0.4	9th	noon 9pm	Division closed BOISLEUX 9am and opened FOSSES FARM. Cable Rear Bde lines very bad. Ringing impossible, speaking almost impossible. Lines overhauled and made D8 throughout. Magnets surging now possible. Superimposed sounder to 162 Bde Visual Station at MONCHY now through to 72 Bde. Wireless through from Div to Bdes.	MB.
	10th		Overhaul of lines continued. Signal Office moved to more secure ... Superimposed sounder to 169 Bde	MB.

WAR DIARY or INTELLIGENCE SUMMARY

Army Form C. 2118.

Page 3 SEPTEMBER 1918

56th Divl. Signal Coy RE (T)

Place	Date	Hour	Summary of Events and Information	Remarks and references to Appendices
FOSSES FARM	11th		2/Lieut TITCHMARSH returned. Lieut PARKINSON (169 Bde) - on leave. Capt. WYBREW 8th Middx relieved Lieut Boë (167 Bde) - on leave. Intermediate Visual Station established at BOIS DU VERT under Cpl Polyblank.	Nil.
N.12.a.0.4	12th		Cpl Page and part of MX-HX bury - also between enemy coys box at present. Bird Dvrch g station (Kneller) moved to VIS-EN-ARTOIS. Comn D.S. moved to FOSSES FARM	Nil.
	13th		2/Lieut Scarlett continued to pair & spiral Route June FOSSES FM to VIS-EN-ARTOIS making use of German permanent line. Cpl Page continued HM bury.	Nil.
	14th		Working parties as yesterday. 167 Bde relieved 168 Bde (all right) and moved Hqrs to PIG & J.S. 168 Bde went to Support Hq at H.25.a.8.3 instead of ARRAS.	Nil.
	15th		Working parties as yesterday	Nil.

WAR DIARY
INTELLIGENCE SUMMARY.

Page 4. SEPTEMBER 1918 Army Form C. 2118.

50th Signal Coy. R.E. (T.)

Place	Date	Hour	Summary of Events and Information	Remarks and references to Appendices
FOSSES FARM	16th		Silent leave continued hop pole route to VIS-EN-ARTOIS. Cpl Langley continued. HM lorry. Warning order received that 4th Xn will relieve 11th Div on our left, and also our left Bde. he will side slip and relieve 3rd Cdn Div on right Bde.	MA
	17th		TQ Cable Pair Quento and TQ Linesman moved to SC.	MA
	18th		2nd Heavy lorry laid two pairs of Cables from Left Bn Hd. Bde. to P34.a.2.8. One pair from IC to O.21d.6.5. to HQ Hd. Bde. 15th Inf. Bde. (4th Div) relieved 167 Hd Bde. 16th Inf. Bde. relieved 119 Hd Bde. 167 Hd Bde took over from 8th Cdn Inf. Bde. frontage of Left Battn.	} B.
	19th		Advanced Exchange established at REMY O.18.c.6.6. At 51 SWM.) - Test at SC Class I switchclip and DH b/h pack continued. SA portion between FOSSES FARM and TP established and in action. Work completed. Cable as far as REMY. TQ Rewrd Factory circled on to SC. HM dam running REMY Mb. Cavalry and K Cyps H relieved Div.	MA

WAR DIARY / INTELLIGENCE SUMMARY

Army Form C. 2118.

Page 5 Sept 1918. 56th Divl. Sig. Coy. R.E.(T)

Place	Date	Hour	Summary of Events and Information	Remarks and references to Appendices
FOSSEUX	Sept 1st		Visited H.Q. Canadian Inf. Bde. Nbr. & Villers Cagnicourt area. Catt began overhaul. Telns had lib. Instd. CNO HQrs.	Nil
F.A.M.	2nd		Turn table cabs moved.	
			Carried out school of activity of Artillery functions. Reconnoitred VILLERS CAGNICOURT — BARALLE area. Exchange at REMY closed. HQrs 189 Inf Bde to pull poles down. Returned to relay wire HQrs 169 (Canadian Inf Bde).	Nil
	3rd		Linesmen out at 9 am to relay. Recovery in prog. YEFR begun. Ret. 4/11 6.Co. HQr. H 19 d 4.1.	
			(126.8). Sent a van to K.... YEFR H. 19 Inf Bde D. YEFR & H 19 d 4.1.	
			Vans out. Sword wagon. "G-6" CLH.Q. 169 Y B F	
			at YEFR. Advanced party of Sig. & YEFR	Nil
	5th		Forwd cable conection established between YEFR & Battn HQrs	
			167 & 169 Inf Bde. Prov. exchanges (Q.a.o.3) & WPCo.8). Mower had	
			been to YEFR & WPCo.8 (2) & Rocket... Our Direct.... WPCo -	Nil
			ECOURTONNE. Second relay at VILLERS CAGNICOURT.	
			An O.R. to Hospital. 1 Officer sent to YEFR.	
	6th		Established Fwd Station HQrs/167 & 169 Inf Bdes into	
			Q.19.5 forward to 8 a 2.0 from 4 am. 166 was also into	
			FOSSIER FARM.	
			HQrs 169 Inf Bde established Hill Batt HQr. WPC.o.8	
	6pm		169 Inf Bde established Hd. Batt HQrs (Q.a.o.3.3.1)	Nil

WAR DIARY or INTELLIGENCE SUMMARY

Army Form C. 2118.

PAGE 6.

SEPT 1918

56th DIV. SIG. COY (R.E.)

Place	Date	Hour	Summary of Events and Information	Remarks and references to Appendices
V36.L.8.	27th	4.30 AM	Artillery and Cable attack used. Left 169 to 169 Inf Bde at BARAGE LAYOUT.	
		5.0 AM	Encountered	
		7.0 AM	Two lines to Canadian Corps	
			Ment to Subsequent Centre for 169 at W.O.C. H.Q. reopened.	
		5.0 PM	169 took of Hq of 169 & 168 Inf Bde attached	
		7.30 PM	169 Inf Bde Hqrs opened at WANCOURT FARM (W.10.C.N.8) communication by line (aerial) and trencher & wire laying) during the day. 168 Inf Bde S.S. Moved back to posn established at D.28.c.3.0 at C.M.	160
	28th		Wire laid between 168 & 169 Inf Bde between 168 and 169 Inf Bde. Wires between 168 & 169 Inf Bde though mainly up to O.Bde H.Q's two lines established from Inf Brigade Forward Communications Centre between O.Pip's & Bu Hqrs Transmitting station at BARAGE QUARRY.	161
	29th	4.30 AM	2 wires of Rel of H to Inf and 169 Inf Bde wanted to be relieved by a Rel of H [unclear] Div were held. Buzzer R [unclear] to their position of 169 Bde H.Q. at O.34 R.4.5. Move of Rear Bde H.Q. from LES FOSSES FARM to VILLERS CARNIEUX and completed. Telephone took over from Inf ? Telegraph and to be from Capt My....	

WAR DIARY
INTELLIGENCE SUMMARY.
(Erase heading not required.)

Army Form C. 2118.

PAGE 7

September 1918

57th Divisional Sig. Coy. R.E. (T)

Place	Date	Hour	Summary of Events and Information	Remarks and references to Appendices
Vis / S	30 Army		169 Inf. Bde. found new HQrs at O.24d.3.6. Line laid between WANCOURT FARM & 167/169 Inf. Bde. Also between 169 & 168 Inf. Bdes. 168 Inf. Bde. moved to ingress to MARQUION pm learned that they had not. (W16 & 6.5) lines laid running taking wires from Bn. Sub. Stn. to NARELLE FARM & PITS & new HQrs of 168 Inf. Bde. & long lines from WANCOURT FARM & "J" Div. HQrs. 11 PM 168 Inf. Bde. decide to go to WANCOURT FARM + lines altered accordingly. Action taken added at midnight	Nil

[signature]
.... MAJOR,
COMMANDING 56th DIVISIONAL SIGNAL COY. R.E.

Army Form C. 2118.

WAR DIARY
or
INTELLIGENCE SUMMARY.
(Erase heading not required.)

PAGE 1 Oct. 1918
55th Bn. 4 Bde A.I.F.
W.D. 33

Place	Date	Hour	Summary of Events and Information	Remarks and references to Appendices
13/10/18	12th		At WIANCOURT FARM. Bn. held front from Road Bel to 160 Inf Bde Hqs.	
		10AM	Insp. 4 posts & B.H.Q. Posts seemed thin & thin on ground. 1 W.O & Corpl sent to find reliable 73, 74 WIANCOURT FARM. Forward communication also established between the Bn. & Bn. H.Q. Battns. either side at WIANCOURT QUARRY. Proposed that H.Q Bn. would be moving to B.H.Q 25 during next 24 hours.	
		10PM	Inspected defences, 116 Inf. Bn. at X.I.C 1.6. Known trench in ... Arrangements with Bde ... 107 Bn. would move to Q 20. B.H.Q. ... and Bn. at the P.O.W. ground at N.E. of Q.9.5.7	M
		11.30AM	C.O went round WIANCOURT FARM ... with the O/C ... here.	
			Recd. from Coy. Cmd. WF. 6 160 I Bde B.G.S. in a return ...	
		2PM	K9 b1 + W9 b4 ... M 2 b3 ... 034 c36 9 ... Hd 119 M + M65 ... low Dimo Buffs. WIANCOURT FARM exchange to M16 SSE. Into Bn. HQ. Being closed. ... cover ... Kenning of lines ...	M

WAR DIARY / INTELLIGENCE SUMMARY

Army Form C. 2118.

Page 2. OCTOBER 1918
56th Divl. Signal Coy RE (T.)

Place	Date	Hour	Summary of Events and Information	Remarks and references to Appendices
V26/15 VILLERS-AU-FLOS	4th		One party commenced poling RW 2 from SP to WF. Cpl Heppell and party seeded up old lines from REMY to BOURLON WOOD.	ML
	5th		167 Inf Bde relieved 169 Inf Bde on Left Sector at 1800 Hours. Cable from SP to WF (Airline RW 2) - continued poling. Lines from WF to 167 Bde posts on trees.	ML
	6th		Cpl Sparks finished poling RW2. Changes to winter time at 0100 this morning.	ML
	7th		Signal Artel buses given ETRUN to AGNEZ-LES-DUISANS.	ML
	8th		General maintenance.	ML
	9th		Cable lines to Divl Train Hqrs at V.1.a.2.3.	ML
	10th		Nil.	
	11th		169 Inf Bde Sig Sup. Relieves 168 Inf Bde on Right Sector this evening.	ML
			56th Divn transferred to Canadian Corps. General maintenance.	
	12th		167 Inf Bde Hqrs moves to Q.23.c.9.6. 10th Can Inf Bde moves w/o 167 & 169 Inf Bdes. A cross cable detachment sent to NAMEOUT? from 169 Inf Bde.	ML
			RFA moved to HAMEL - no telephone communication at present.	ML

WAR DIARY
INTELLIGENCE SUMMARY.
(Erase heading not required.)

Army Form C. 2118.

Page 3.   OCTOBER 1918.   56th Divl. Signal Coy R.E.

Place	Date	Hour	Summary of Events and Information	Remarks and references to Appendices
VILLERS-LES-CAGNICOURT	14th		168 Inf Bde moved to ARRAS. Communication through ARRAS exchange. Line put through to 155 RFA Army Bde at 16.00 hours.	MM
	15th		10th Canl Inf Bde relieved 169 Bde last night. 169 Inf Bde moved to HAUTE AVESNES today.	MM
ETRUN	16th		Divn HQrs closed VILLERS CAGNICOURT 10 a.m. opened ETRUN chateau same hour. 167 Inf Bde relieved by 12th Canl Inf Bde and moves to Y huts on the ARRAS - ST. POL Road. Phone & Sounder communication to all three Brigades.	MM
	17th		Overhauling and Clearing up.	MM
	18th		M.T. Coy moved from ROEUX WOOD to MAROEUIL and connected to Divl Exchange.	MM
	19th 20th 21st		Re-equipping Detachments. Revd Draft 1st/1st Midlothian Regt (A.L.) posted to 1st Army Signal Coy and attached for duty.	MM MM
	22nd		Overhauling equipment.	MM
	23rd		Cable Wagon Drill - Training	MM

WAR DIARY
INTELLIGENCE SUMMARY.
(Erase heading not required.)

Army Form C. 2118.

Page 4. OCTOBER 1918. 56th Divl. Signal Coy. R.E. (T).

Place	Date	Hour	Summary of Events and Information	Remarks and references to Appendices
ETRUN	24th		General cleaning up – Horses – Harness – wagons and equipment.	Nil.
	25th			
	26th			
	27th			
	28th			
	29th			
	30th		Warning order received that Division will move to BASSEVILLE tomorrow. Billets N.E. of CAMBRAI.	Nil.
BASSEVILLE	31st		Division transferred from Canadian Corps to XVII Corps – closed at ETRUN and opened at BASSEVILLE 10.30 hours. 167 and 168 Bdes at DOUCHY, connects to 49th Div Exchange. 169 Bde at LIEU ST. AMAND connects to Div by cable/wireless.	Nil.

M Ranyard
MAJOR,
COMMANDING 56th DIVISIONAL SIGNAL COY. R.E.

Army Form C. 2118.

WAR DIARY
or
INTELLIGENCE SUMMARY.
(Erase heading not required.)

Vol 34

Instructions regarding War Diaries and Intelligence Summaries are contained in F. S. Regs., Part II. and the Staff Manual respectively. Title pages will be prepared in manuscript.

56th. DIVISIONAL SIGNAL COMPANY, R.E., T.F.

NOVEMBER 1918

Place	Date	Hour	Summary of Events and Information	Remarks and references to Appendices
BASEVILLE	1st		SHEET 1. 167 and 168 Brigades at DOUCHY. - Communication via advanced 22nd Corps Exchange and 49th Division Exchange at AVESNES LE SEC. 169 Brigade at LIEU ST AMAND connected to 56th Division direct. Company transport under 2/Lieut. Leavey arrived from Rieux.	ML
MONCHAUX	2nd		Three cable detachments left BASEVILLE for MONCHAUX at 0710 hours, remainder of transport with Sergt. Slodden at 0800. One detachment laid a pair from MONCHAUX to CAUMONT FARM for 168 and 169 Brigades. One detachment laid a pair from MONCHAUX to MAING for 167 Brigade. Divisional Headquarters opened at MONCHAUX at 1500 hours, all three Brigades at MAING on 169 Brigade Exchange. Two pairs from VHP to 169 Brigade Exchange.	ML
	3rd		56th. Division to move front from 49th. Division at 1000 hours - 14th Brigade (49th.Division) on left. - Headquarters MAING - connected direct to VHP. 16th Brigade in centre - Headquarters CAUMONT FARM - 169 Brigade on right - Headquarters CAUMONT FARM. Sounder working to 168 and 169 Brigades at CAUMONT FARM. 167 Brigade in support at MAING connected to 14th Brigade Exchange. Company transport and cable detachments with Captain Aldridge and 2/Lieut. Leavey moved to PANARS.	ML
PANARS	4th		Divisional Headquarters opened at PANARS Chateau at 1000. One cable detachment laid a pair to SAULZAIN for 168 and 169 Brigades. Lines to 14th. Division on the right and 4th. Canadian Division on the left. 167 Brigade moved to AULNOY. One cable detachment laid a pair to AULNOY.	ML
SAULZAIN	4th		Divisional Headquarters closed PANARS 1700 and opened at SAULZAIN same hour. Lines to 168 and 169 Brigades in the village. Line to 167 Brigade in support also in SAULZAIN. 14th Division also laid lateral to SAULZAIN. One detachment laid a line to VALENCIENNES as lateral to 4th Canadian Division. 2/Lieut. Leavey laid line with one detachment from SAULZAIN to SEBOURG for 169 Brigade.	ML

Army Form C. 2118.

WAR DIARY
or
INTELLIGENCE SUMMARY.
(Erase heading not required.)

Instructions regarding War Diaries and Intelligence Summaries are contained in F.S. Regs., Part II. and the Staff Manual respectively. Title pages will be prepared in manuscript.

Place	Date	Hour	Summary of Events and Information	Remarks and references to Appendices
	1918		168 and 169 Brigades moved to GEBOUG. Lieut.McIvor with two detachments sent to 168 Brigade Headquarters to form /4th advanced Exchange. One detachment laid line from GAULLAIN to GEBOUG. Rail through to 4th. Canadian Division at VALENCIENNES.	NC
			168 moved from 169 Brigade Headquarters to STROEUG Chateau (168 Brigade Headquarters) Corps met detachment Teleid paid from GAULLAIN to STROEUG Chateau. Superimposed sounded working to VEN Two and VE . G.69.Divisional Headquarters opened at GAULLAIN at 1800 hours connected to 168 Brigade. 169 Brigade (63rd Division) opened at SEBOURQUIAK at now connected to 63rd.	NC
			167 Brigade laid lines to 169 Brigade on right, 189 Brigade believed 168 Brigade on left. Left Section 168 pss lines to 63rd.Division. 167 Brigade pavel Headquarters to A.GRLAU from GEBOUG. Divisional Headquarters opened at SEBOURG Chateau at 1200 hours. 167 Brigade moved to GN.2218 at 1800 hours - pair extended from AMERSAU to ORANGIES & Corpl. Way all. Norling superimposed sounded to 167 Brigade. 63rd.Division two to DROMOUNTAIN - lateral through at 0-15 8th. L/A.Hearq at VEN., AUTHLAT with two detachments.	NC
			167 Brigade moved to FAYT LE FRANC. One detachment laid from ORANGIES via AUTHLA D to MAIL and FRA C. L/At.Hosver moved FNA and Corpl detachments to AUTHLAE. One detachment laid a line to ALERAE to AMALL as lateral to 65rd.Division. 4th.Division laid lateral to AUTHELAT. Brigade headquarters to imo to FAYT LE FRANC tomorrow. Box car left for WAYT LE FRANC with Signal office and Wireless instruments at 2100 hours.	NC
			Lieut. McIvor Mat Capl Copper Transport at 0100 hours to FAYT LE FRANC. L/Lt.Butcher with two 2lb.N lorry and Wireless personel at 0100. Divisional Headquarters Opened at FAYT LE FRANC at 1000 hours. 189 Brigade had detachment lines to VANEY . One detachment laid earth return circuit to 167 Brigade. 168 Brigade was on No./Maestras . One detachment laid earth return circuit to 168 Brigade. 5th Division laid lateral to MAYT. Headquarters laid out to lat. lat. to 63rd.Division, and 169 Brigade still at AMELLAY - connected to 63rd.	NC

Army Form C. 2118.

WAR DIARY
or
INTELLIGENCE SUMMARY.
(Erase heading not required.)

Instructions regarding War Diaries and Intelligence Summaries are contained in F. S. Regs., Part II. and the Staff Manual respectively. Title pages will be prepared in manuscript.

Place	Date	Hour	Summary of Events and Information	Remarks and references to Appendices
PAVE LE FRANC	Nov 1st 1918		SHEET 3	
	9th		No long traffic possible beyond BOISIN. One detachment laid lateral to 63rd. Division at BLAUGIES.	Nil.
	10th		167 Brigade moved to Quevy le Petit and then on to followed by cable detachments Corps detachment laid pair to QUEVY LE PETIT where VEPK was established under 2n/ Lieut. Malvor with two cable detachments. 168 Brigade moved to NIEU DE BUNY and split new 167 Brigade pair on their exchange. 169 Brigade moved to ATHIS. One detachment laid an earth return circuit to 169 Brigade and levelled up old line to 168 Brigade at ERQUENNES. 190 Brigade (63rd. Division) relieved 167 Brigade. (63rd. Division) ordered to act as advanced guard to 2nd. Corps. 11th. and 56th. Division in support. Pair to YEMA put through at 168 Brigade. 168 Brigade connected on earth circuit to YEPK. Working superimposed YEP to YEM.	Nil.
	11th		One detachment laid line from VEPK to 63rd. Division at the Chateau du Petit Cambrai. Armistice signed with Germany at 1100 hours. Hostilities ceased. 167 Brigade moved back to BOUGNIES. One detachment laid pair from VEMK to BOUGNIES for 167 Brigade. Signal Office moved to the same house as "G" and "Q" Offices. C.R.E. and D.A.P.M. connected to VEP Exchange.	Nil.
	12th		G.T. 168 Relief under Captain Bircher and 1A. Cable Detachment under Sergt.Morris established at YEMK. - QUEVY LE PETIT.	Nil.
	13th		VEPK moved to Farm in AUDREGNIES WC.D, D13z2.6, Sheet 51. 168 Brigade moved to GARD LA BRUYERE Chateau. 167 Brigade moved to QUEVY LE PETIT.3 Line from YAMK to 167 and 168 Brigades and a pair from VEMK to VEP superimposed.	Nil.
	14th		VEMK Working Superimposed to 167 and 168 Brigades.	Nil.
	15th		M.G.Battalion moved from QUEVY LE PETIT to ELAUGIES. No 5 Section laid a pair to Divisional Exchange at PAVE LE FRANC. 416th.Field Company connected to 168 Brigade Exchange and 512th. Field Company connected to VEMK Exchange.	Nil.

SHEET 4.

Army Form C. 2118.

WAR DIARY
or
INTELLIGENCE SUMMARY.
(Erase heading not required.)

Instructions regarding War Diaries and Intelligence Summaries are contained in F. S. Regs., Part II. and the Staff Manual respectively. Title pages will be prepared in manuscript.

Place	Date	Hour	Summary of Events and Information	Remarks and references to Appendices
MAUBEUGE	Nov. 16		The D.A.D.O.S. in MAUBEUGE connected by No.5 Section to the 56th.M.G.Battalion Exchange. Housing and overhauling equipment continued.	Nil.
	17.		Nil.	Nil.
	18.		Overhauling and re-equipping continued.	Nil.
	19.		169 Brigade Headquarters moved from ATHIS to PLAUGIES. Communication via 56th.Battalion M.G. Exchange. 1/5th.Cheshire Regiment connected to the old 169 Brigade line.	Nil.
	20.			Nil.
	21.		Refitting and re-painting wagons.	Nil.
	22.		Warning order received that Division will move shortly to 63rd.Divisional Area South of MONS.	Nil.
	23.		Two pairs L.16 line from the ATHIS - DOUR road to pick up the Corps airline route, and release the cable to ATHIS.	Nil.
	24.		A.D.M.S. Corps moved to MONS at 1200 noon. Communication from YDF to two pairs of cable to airline route on ATHIS - DOUR road, thence on airline pair 1/2, Eastwards to Corps at MONS, and Westwards via the D.A.D.O.S.	Nil.
	25.		167 Brigade Headquarters moved from QUEVY LE PETIT to QUEVY LE GRAND. Communication via old 1st Essex signal office at QUEVY LE PETIT. Conference on Education Scheme held at Headquarters 167 Brigade at 1415 hours.	Nil.
	26.			Nil.
	27.		168 Brigade Headquarters moved from PLAUGIES to HARVENG. Communication via 63rd.Division Exchange. 169 Brigade Headquarters moved from SARS LA BRUYERE to GIVRY. Communication via G316.	Nil.
	28.		Division Headquarters closed at PAYS LE FRANC at 1100 hours and opened at TAVERN GIVRY. 9th Battalion H.L.I. Section hooked up the D.S pair from TAVERN to QUEVY.	Nil. 1.4009.0

D. D. & L., London, E.C.

Army Form C. 2118.

WAR DIARY
or
INTELLIGENCE SUMMARY.   SHEET 5.

(Erase heading not required.)

Instructions regarding War Diaries and Intelligence Summaries are contained in F. S. Regs., Part II. and the Staff Manual respectively. Title pages will be prepared in manuscript.

Place	Date	Hour	Summary of Events and Information	Remarks and references to Appendices
	Nov 1. 25th. (Contd.)		LES PETIT. CREVY LE GRAND and HARVENG. The other detachment of 1.A.Section laid a pair of cables from 167 Brigade Headquarters at CREVY LE GRAND to HARVENG. Communication by 1600 hours as follows:- 167 Brigade .... Cable 168 Brigade .... Cable and Permanent Route via HARVENG. 169 Brigade .... Cable.	AV.
	29th.		NIL	AV.
HARVENG	30th.		169 Brigade Headquarters moved from HARVENG to NOUVELLES. An existing pair of D.3 cable picked up from HARVENG to NOUVELLES. Details of Christmas dinners settled at a Company conference.	AV.

M. Rainford
Major,
O.C. A.E.
J.C. Signals
56th Division.

DECEMBER 1918.   Page 1.   56th Divl Signal Co.
WAR DIARY
INTELLIGENCE SUMMARY.
Army Form C. 2118.

R.E. T.F. (2/1st London)

90 35

Place	Date	Hour	Summary of Events and Information	Remarks and references to Appendices
HARVENG	Dec 1st	1800	Communications as follows. 167 Bde at QUEVY-LE-GRAND - cable pair	M/R
			168 Bde at GIVRY, cable pair to HARMIGNIES, thence Permaline pair to GIVRY	M/R
	2nd		Hq 2 Div at NOUVELLES - cable pair	
			Day spent in making comfort of billets and in talking at NOUVELLES + HAINY	M/R
	3rd		Am. Two sigs. sent to RUEIL, MONS	M/R
	4th		Later had 8 more sent to visit MONS. 18 Och. walked on the Rue Fere	M/R
	5th		All issued to the outlying sapper lines - While round	M/R
	6th			M/R
	7th		Nil.	M/R
	8th			M/R
	9th		All Coy. Personnel ranks recovered with a view to salvage	
			cable par't. Went to LONGUEAU to hand in cable.	
	10th			
	11th		Nil.	
	12th			
	13th			

December 1918. Page 2.

WAR DIARY
INTELLIGENCE SUMMARY

56th (1st London) Divl. Signal Coy. R.E. T.F.

Army Form C. 2118.

(Erase heading not required.)

Place	Date	Hour	Summary of Events and Information	Remarks and references to Appendices
HARVENG.	15th	1800	Nil	AM
	16th		1A Sect. working on mains to DAC and 16 London Regt. 1B Sect. working on line to 167 Bde.	AM
	17th		No 5 Section withdrawn from 56 M.G. Batt. and Gilletta with the Corporas at HARVENG. 1A and 1B Sections as yesterday. New Cinema Building erected from HARVENG for the main MUSIC-HALL series road. Lieutenant Parkinson and Corp. Quint leaving MM awarded Military Crosses.	AM
	18th		1A and 1B Sections continued repairing door route along the Mons-Maubeuge Road. No 5 Sect. commenced digging pole holes for route reconn'd yesterday.	AM
	19th		1A and 1B as yesterday	AM
	20th			
	21st		Nil	AM
	22nd			AM
	23rd		1A and 1B Sects carried on with work on Mons-Maubeuge route	AM
	24th		Nil	AM
	25th		Xmas Day. Company Dinner held at 1330 hours. Company Concert held at 1900.	AM

DECEMBER 1918

WAR DIARY 56th Divl. (1st London) Signal Coy. R.E. T.F.
Page 3.
INTELLIGENCE SUMMARY.

Army Form C. 2118.

Place	Date	Hour	Summary of Events and Information	Remarks and references to Appendices
HARVENG	26th	1830	NIL - "A" Company third Divve organised	Nil.
	27th		1st Div. linked up to 168 Bde Giuy. No 5 Section finished rigging up	Nil.
			Pole route on new permanent route.	
	28th		NIL	Nil.
	29th			Nil.
	30th		1st A Sect commenced diverting two pair airline to the 16th London Regt	Nil.
			at Givry and to the 283rd Army Bde R.F.A. at NOIRCHAIN.	
	31st		1st Sect on yesterday.	Nil.

....
M Ramsey?
MAJOR,
COMMANDING 56th DIVISIONAL SIGNAL COY. R.E.

56

Signal Coy

Vol II

January 1919. Page 1

Army Form C. 2118.

WAR DIARY
or
INTELLIGENCE SUMMARY.

56th (1/1st London) Div. Signal Company R.E. T.F.

(Erase heading not required.)

Instructions regarding War Diaries and Intelligence Summaries are contained in F. S. Regs., Part II. and the Staff Manual respectively. Title pages will be prepared in manuscript.

WO 36

Place	Date	Hour	Summary of Events and Information	Remarks and references to Appendices
HARVENG	Jan 1st 1919		Company later classified by RADVS as X, Y or Z. 1a cable Section complete the diversion of the Mar-beny airline route to the 282nd Bray Bde RFA and the 1/16th London Regt (Q.W.Rifles)	All
	2nd		1B announced scrambler 3 pair General route from AVRY to VILLERS-SIRE-NICOLE	AR
	3rd		1B of yesterday 1A laid in new pair aerial route from HARVENG NON-L'EVEQUE (road) with the Signal Office	All
	4th		NIL	All
	5th		NIL	
	6th		1B invited out VILLERS SIRE NICOLE route 1a by HARVENG-HOUDENG-NOVELLE Road to 1b	AR
	7th		1A As yesterday. 1b put pair Trunks to QUEVY-le-GRAND for the 1/12th London Regt	All
	8th		1B, 1st Visits pair 1A to 56 Bde and No1 Coy 3rd Div Train	AR
	9th		NIL	
	10th		No 1 Sec laid up D2 wire between HARVENG and QUEVY-LE-GRAND	All

(5975) Wt W23587/30 60000 12/17. D.D.& L. Sch 3a. Forms/C2118/15

January 1919. Page 2. WAR DIARY 56th (2/1st London) Divl. Signal Company R.E., T.F.
INTELLIGENCE SUMMARY. Army Form C. 2118.

Place	Date	Hour	Summary of Events and Information	Remarks and references to Appendices
HARVENG	Jan 11th		NIL	? FMC
	12th		NIL	? FMC
	13th		No.5 Section reeled up cables to 282nd Army Brigade R.F.A. at NOIRCHAIN and to the D.A.C. at CIPLY. 1A Section connected Divl. Train Company at MESVIN to the Exchange. 1B connected to 2nd London Reg and 5th London Regt both at HARMIGNIES to the Exchange.	M.
	14th		Work as yesterday.	M.
	15th		No.5 Section collected 8-way ams from the German took at CIPLY	M.
	16th		No.5 Section as yesterday.	M.
	17th		1A, 1B, No.5 Sect and the RA Section commenced repairing the Civilian Railway route from SPIENNES to HARMIGNIES.	M.
	18th		Work as yesterday.	M.
	19th		Church Parade	M.
	20th		No.5 Section commenced putting a third pair on the HARVENG – NOUVELLES – MEURBERGE road route. 1A, 1B and the RA Sect finished the railway route from SPIENNES to HARMIGNIES.	M.

January 1919. Page 3. 56th (1st London) Div. Army Form C. 2118.

WAR DIARY / INTELLIGENCE SUMMARY.

Signal Company R.E. T.F.

(Erase heading not required.)

Place	Date	Hour	Summary of Events and Information	Remarks and references to Appendices
HARVENG	21st (1919)		No 5 Section finished aerial covered yesterday. 1B Section put a test fault in the transport route at the Sugar Factory on the GIVRY – RAVAI road, near GIVRY.	A/19
	22nd		RA Section commenced cleaning damaged cables in HARVENG.	A/16
	23rd		RA Section as yesterday. 1B put a test point on the Mons – Maubeuge road route 14 (route 1A uses) between the GIVRY – FRAMERIES and GIVRY – RAVAI road cross roads.	A/17
	24th		No 5 Section continued cleaning up lines in HARVENG. Cable work to Mons – Maubeuge road route 14 at the GIVRY – RAVAI cross roads. 1A, 1B, 160 Bde RFA at GOEGNIES CHAUSSÉE. RA and No 5 Sections as yesterday.	A/18
	25th		Lectured on 1A's end.	A/19
	26th		Nil	B/11
	27th		No 5 Section as on 24 & 25. RA Section continued moving cables to QUÉVY LE PETIT. 1A and 1B Sections were given N.B. Command Signal at MYON.	J/1

January 1919 Page 4

WAR DIARY
INTELLIGENCE SUMMARY

56th (1st London) Divl. Signal Company RE. T.F.

Army Form C. 2118.

Place	Date	Hour	Summary of Events and Information	Remarks and references to Appendices
HARVENG	28th		Work as yesterday.	MC
	29th		RA Section as yesterday. 1A 1B & D S Sections Cleared HARVENG and returned to 1/4 Qrs. All Y and Z group horses given medicines last 5/6 glanders	MC
	30th		Work as yesterday. Horses evacuated	MC
	31st		Work as yesterday	MC

M Kaye?
Major RE
O.C. 56th (1/1st London) Divl. Signal
Coy. RE. TF.

February 1919. Part 1. 56th (2/1st London) Divnl Signal Company R.E. (T.F.)

Army Form C. 2118.

WAR DIARY
or
INTELLIGENCE SUMMARY.
(Erase heading not required.)

Instructions regarding War Diaries and Intelligence Summaries are contained in F.S. Regs., Part II. and the Staff Manual respectively. Title pages will be prepared in manuscript.

Place	Date	Hour	Summary of Events and Information	Remarks and references to Appendices
HARVENG (BELGIUM)	Feb 1		Nil	
	2		Nil	
	3		56 S.S. returned and sent cable to HARVENG	
	4		Nil	
	5		CSO 1st Army signed that no demobilisation	
	6			
	7			
	8			
	9			

WAR DIARY

INTELLIGENCE SUMMARY

Army Form C. 2118.

February 1919 Page 2

50 (Northumbrian) Divnl Signal Coy RE

Place	Date	Hour	Summary of Events and Information	Remarks and references to Appendices
HARVENG (BELGIUM)	17		Nil	SEE
	18		Nil	SEE
	19		Nil	SEE
	20		Nil	SEE
	21	Draft of 53 ORs posted to 4th Army signal 20 posted to 2nd Army	SEE
	22			SEE
	23		Nil	SEE
	24		Nil	SEE
	25		Nil	SEE
	26		Nil	SEE
	27		Nil	SEE
	28		Nil	SEE

S.B. Mitchell
Lt.Col. 50 Divnl Sig Coy RE

MARCH 1919 Page 1.

Army Form C. 2118.

WAR DIARY
INTELLIGENCE SUMMARY.
(Erase heading not required.)

56th (2/1st London) Divl. Signal Coy. R.E. T.F.

Appx 38

Place	Date	Hour	Summary of Events and Information	Remarks and references to Appendices
HARVENG	1st		Nil.	M2
"	2nd		Capt. Bro. ALDRIDGE M.C. R.E. T.F. left unit for demobilisation.	M2
"	3rd		10 hrs. left for demob.	M2
"	4th			
"	5th		Nil	M2
"	6th			
"	7th		8 hrs. left for demob.	M2
"	8th		Nil.	M2
"	9th		9 hrs. left for demob.	M2
"	10th			M2
"	11th		Nil	M2
"	12th			
"	13th		6 hrs. left for demobilisation	M2
"	14th		Unit now reduced cadre strength reduced to Cadre "A"	42
"	15th		Nil	M2

WAR DIARY

INTELLIGENCE SUMMARY

March 1919, Page 2. Army Form C. 2118.

56th (2/1st London) Divl. Signal Coy, R.E., T.F.

Place	Date	Hour	Summary of Events and Information	Remarks and references to Appendices
HARVENG Belgium	17th		Nil	
"	18th		Party starts clearing HARVENG of unused cables	All
"	19th		Orders issued to evacuate all operators R. Switchbd OPs. from Linesmen and DRs	All
"	20th	10am	All above returned for 2nd Army. GNRY (abor) & Cables	All
"	21st		QUEVY-LE-GRAND cleared of cable	All
"	22nd		VIEUX RENG and ROUVEROY cleared of cables. 281 BDE R.F.A. moved to QUESMES	All
"	23rd		GRAND RENG and VILLERS SRE NICOLE cleared of cables	All
"	24th		HARMIGNIES cleared of cable also lines from Nouvelle to Spiennes (cables)	All
"	25th		168 Bde moves to CUESMES. QUEVY-LE-PETIT cleared of cables	All
"	26th		GOEGNIES CHAUSSEE cleared of cables. 280 Bde R.F.A. moved to FLENU	All
"	27th		ASQUILLIES cleared of cables. 513 Fd Coy moved to JEMAPPES	All
"	28th		M.T. Lines to HARVENG closed except Office and RAH9	All
"	29th		All remaining cables having to Jemappes ready for withdrawal	All
JEMAPPES Belgium	29th		Two men demobbed. HQrs Dvl. Sigs moved to Jemappes	All
"	30th		Local lines laid in Jemappes. Army withdrawn. HQrs 280 R.G. R.F.A.	All
	31/4/19			56 Div (2/1st London) Div Sig Coy R.E., T.F.

April 1919 Page 1 WAR DIARY Army Form C. 2118.

56th (2/1st London) Divl. Signal Coy. R.E. T.F.

WSC 39

Place	Date	Hour	Summary of Events and Information	Remarks and references to Appendices
Jenappes	April 1st	1830	Telephone pair arranged direct to 281 & 282 Bde RFA at MERVIN, via Quievrain	AAC
	2nd		281 Bde RFA put on to London Exchange at Quievrain. Their line being used to connect the 4th London to the Divl Exchange at Jenappes.	AAC
	3rd		281 and 282 Bdes RFA bunched 16 Corps Exchange. RA HQrs and DAC also bunched to Corps Exchange. Lieuts McIver and Clark left for 2nd [illeg] Divl. Signal Coy.	AAC
	4th		Wagon lines moving. All RE Signal personnel withdrawn from 166 Inf Bde and from 281 Bde RFA. All Coy personnel now at Jenappes	AAC
	5th			
	6th		Nil	AAC
	7th			
	8th			
	9th		One vacancy for demobilisation received	AAC
	10th		Party commenced clearing up derelict cable in Jenappes	AAC
	11th		6 vacancies for demobilisation. Clearing up Jenappes continued	AAC
	12th		All demobilisation work now ceased	AAC

April 1919   Page 2.

WAR DIARY 56th (1st London) Div. Signal Coy. R.E. T.F

Army Form C. 2118.

INTELLIGENCE SUMMARY

(Erase heading not required.)

Place	Date	Hour	Summary of Events and Information	Remarks and references to Appendices
Jenappes.	April 13th	1830	Nil.	AM.
	14th		9 vacancies for demobilisation received.	AM.
	15th		Nil.	AM.
	16th		Orders received to strip and oil all harness. Harness to be packed in company park.	AM.
	17th		Harness cleaning.	AM.
	18th		Good Friday.	AM.
	19th		Route march to Bois DE GHLIN. Dinners and Teas served in the wood.	AM.
	20th		Easter Sunday.	AM.
	21st		Nil.	AM.
	22nd		Harness stripping and cleaning continued.	AM.
	23rd		Lorry equipment overhauled. Harness as yesterday.	AM.
	24th		Harness cleaning.	AM.
	25th		Harness cleaning.	AM.
	26th		Harness cleaning. RA HQ moved from HARVENG to Mons Maubeuge Road near Ciply. O/6 cable in Harveng lashed up. Tea put in for new HQ.	AM.

April 1919. Page 3.

WAR DIARY 56th (2/1st London)
INTELLIGENCE SUMMARY. Divl. Signal Coy. R.E. T.F.

Army Form C. 2118.

Place	Date	Hour	Summary of Events and Information	Remarks and references to Appendices
Chaples	April 27th	1830	RDAQ run at Q.3.e.2.4.9.	Nil
	28th		Harness cleaning continued.	Nil
	29th			
	30th			

M Ransford
MAJOR,
COMMANDING 56th DIVISIONAL SIGNAL COY. R.E.

Army Form C. 2118.

WAR DIARY
or
INTELLIGENCE SUMMARY.
(Erase heading not required.)

MAY 1919

Sgt U. Dw Eng. Coy.

Instructions regarding War Diaries and Intelligence Summaries are contained in F. S. Regs., Part II. and the Staff Manual respectively. Title pages will be prepared in manuscript.

Place	Date	Hour	Summary of Events and Information	Remarks and references to Appendices
Genappes	1		Men ethier sent to for demobilization.	
	2-6		Nothing to report.	
	7		Three men demobilized, the remained the cadre strength.	
	8			
	9		Major A.T. RANSFORD proceeded to S.M.E. Chatham, Lt E.H. COE	
			M.C. assumed command	
	10-11		Nothing of interest	
	12		Warning order for return received	
	13-17		Preparations for departure	
	18		Entrained Entire Entrained for Antwerp	
Antwerp	19		On cadre arrived at Antwerp. Handed supplies to cadre.	
	20-25		Parades, mount inspection etc	
	26		Cadre embarked on S.S. Sicilian	
Albury	28		" disembarked at Tilbury	
Ripon	29		" arrived at Ripon Camp	
	30-31		Nothing to report	

www.ingramcontent.com/pod-product-compliance
Lightning Source LLC
Chambersburg PA
CBHW080855230426
43662CB00013B/2108